P9-BIB-072

THE REFORMATION

THE REFORMATION

Revival or Revolution?

Edited by **W. STANFORD REID**

University of Guelph

HOLT, RINEHART AND WINSTON

New York · Chicago · San Francisco · Atlanta
Dallas · Montreal · Toronto · London

Cover illustration: A group of Reformation leaders, painting by Lucas Cranach. Those featured are Luther (left foreground), Erasmus (fourth from right), and Melanchthon (far right). (Epitaph from the altar of Meienburg; *Bettmann Archive*).

Copyright © 1968 by Holt, Rinehart and Winston, Inc.
All Rights Reserved
Library of Congress Catalog Card Number: 68-28181
ISBN 0-03-071475-3
Printed in the United States of America
456789 008 98765

CAMROSE LUTHERAN COLLEGE
LIBRARY

BR
309
R4 / 34,592

CONTENTS

Introduction   1

PROTESTANT VIEWS OF THE REFORMATION

JEAN HENRI MERLE D'AUBIGNÉ—God's Action in History   9
E. G. LÈONARD—Revival of the Church's Life   13
GERHARD RITTER—Luther's Place in the Reformation   18
E. G. SCHWIEBERT—The Background of the Times   23
GEORGE HUNSTON WILLIAMS—Radical Elements in the
    Reformation   30
ROLAND H. BAINTON—The Complexity of the Reformation   37

THE ROMAN CATHOLIC INTERPRETATION

MARTIN J. SPALDING—Merle d'Aubigné's Views Challenged   46
P. H. GRISAR, S.J.—Tempest in State and Church   51
HUGH ROSS WILLIAMSON—The English Reformation: An
    Expression of Greed   65
GEORGES TAVARD—Similarity Between Reformation
    Doctrines and Catholic Beliefs   72
PIERRE JANELLE—Anarchy: The Disease Within the Church   80

THE SECULAR EXPLANATION

PRESERVED SMITH—Changes in Scientific Knowledge and
    Ethical Feeling   93
EVA PRIESTER—A Socio-economic Phenomenon   98
H. A. E. VAN GELDER—The Renaissance: The True
    Reformation   106
PETER MASTEN DUNNE, S.J.—The Need for Objectivity   112

Suggested Additional Readings   119

The fight between Luther and Calvin, with the Pope in
the background, as portrayed in a contemporary cartoon.
(*Bettmann Archive*)

INTRODUCTION

The Protestant Reformation of the sixteenth century is one of the most complex movements in European history since the fall of the Roman Empire and one of the most difficult to assess. Our understanding of the movement is hampered not only by the wide variety of factors involved but also by the subjective reactions of those writing about it. For this reason, it would seem, many historians have sought to avoid committing themselves to a general interpretation of the religious upheaval. Preserved Smith in the early 1920s indeed deplored the scarcity of all-embracing analyses, and while the situation has improved, the many studies published over the past forty years indicate clearly that historians have by no means reached agreement on the character of the Reformation, what it accomplished, or what it contributed to the development of Western culture.

What is the cause of these differences of perspective? One cannot say that it is the facts, for historians all work with much the same facts. The differences lie in the emphases, weight, and meaning they give to the facts, and their evaluations, in turn, depend on the presuppositions with which they approach the subject. The historian who believes that man's basic motive is religious will deal with the Reformation differently from the historian who holds that the economic motive is fundamental. Their conflicting evaluations of events, statements, and reactions will consequently produce widely divergent explanations.

One does find, despite the many differences, that views on the Reformation fall into three general schools. Protestant historians have, as one might expect, manifested a favorable attitude to the movement, usually holding the Reformation to have been necessary. This interpretation began with Flaccius Illyricus' *Magdeburg Centuries* (1562–1574) and has continued to the present time. The Roman Catholic historians' opposition to this viewpoint first appeared in the *Annales Ecclesiastici* (1588–1607) of Cardinal Baronius who, in defense of the Church of Rome, labeled the Protestants heretics. This position has formed the basis of most Roman Catholic approaches to the Reformation to the present, although it has been modified recently by some writers. Another approach to the movement has regarded the religious aspects

1

as merely surface manifestations. Economic forces, social change, political or nationalistic revolution have all been put forward as the true motives for, and dynamic of, the Reformation, indicating that historians must find its ultimate explanation in secular rather than religious factors. Differences among these schools of thought all have their roots in prior convictions concerning man, the Church, and history itself.

Even within these three groupings there are differences. The Protestants by no means show unity of outlook. Historians within the Lutheran tradition tend to stress Luther and his accomplishments. Those from the Reformed, or Calvinist, churches usually emphasize the work and teaching of Zwingli, Calvin, Cranmer, and Knox. Others, tracing their spiritual origins back to the so-called Radical Reformation of the Anabaptists who disliked both Lutherans and Calvinists almost as much as they did Roman Catholics, feel that the "radical" view of the Reformation is the correct one. Consequently, there is conflict even within the Protestant camp.

Among Roman Catholics less difference exists. Generally they do not believe that the Reformation was "a good thing," but even in this group varying shades of opinion appear. For one thing, in recent years under the influence of ecumenical dialogue with Protestants, the older, harsh judgments of the Reformation have given way to a somewhat more irenic attitude. Protestants are now regarded less as heretics than as "separated brethren." Furthermore, some recent Roman Catholic writers have tended to stress some specific aspect of the Reformation as being of primary importance, but they have not always agreed as to which aspect was most significant.

There is debate, too, among those who favor a "secular" interpretation of the Reformation. This usually goes back to the question of the nature of religion itself and its influence on history. Very early in the Reformation some writers sought to explain the movement in terms of nationalism or the rivalry between the scholars of monastic orders. In the past century or so, as a result of a growing interest in economics and sociology, some historians have sought to use these social sciences to explain its origins and development. Within this school of thought, too, there are varying opinions despite essential agreement that religious motivations were not the ultimate causes and architects of the movement.

The Protestant reformers of the sixteenth century and their immediate followers held that the Reformation was a necessary spiritual revival and reformation of a church which had become almost totally corrupt. This conception received its modern classical statement in the nineteenth-century work of Jean Henri Merle d'Aubigné. His *History of the Reformation* (13 vols.; 1835–1878) has this as its underlying theme, but he expresses it most clearly in the introduction, from which comes the first selection. He declares that the Reformation is a clear demonstration of God's redemptive action in history. At the same time, he recognizes man's part in the drama and seeks to show the relationship of divine and human factors. To him the Reformation was without a doubt good, for it restored to man true religion and consequently true freedom under God. His writings reflect many undertones of nineteenth-century European thought.

The general interpretation expressed by Merle d'Aubigné continues to dominate the thinking of many in the Reformed, or Calvinist, tradition, as may be seen from the title *John Calvin, the Man whom God Called*, a recent work by Jean Cadier, of Montpellier, France. The works of Josef Bohatec of Vienna, especially his *Budé und Calvin*, follow the same pattern. While these writers take careful note of the work of such men as Luther, Calvin, and others, they strongly believe that ultimately the Reformation was, in a special way, divine action in history.

Although following in the same Reformed tradition, E. G. Leonard, represented in the next selection, has more recently introduced a new note. He believes that the Reformation was not actually a breaking away from the medieval Church but rather the true flowering of medieval Christianity. One must ask whether this is the proper understanding of the movement and endeavour to see how this point of view accords not only with other Protestant explanations but also with the Roman Catholic accounts. It does represent a departure from the view usually held by Reformed analysts of the Reformation.

In Lutheran circles one finds a somewhat different emphasis from that in Reformed thought. Although the spiritual descendants of Luther never doubt the divine origins of the Reformation, they concentrate more on the pivotal position of the first reformer, and with good reason. Calvin himself repeatedly refers to Luther as the human originator of the movement. Accordingly, one should not be surprised that in recent years historians not in the direct line of spiritual lineage have also stressed Luther's unique importance. The works of Gordon Rupp, especially *The Righteousness of God*, and Roland H. Bainton's *Here I Stand* demonstrate the non-Lutheran's interest in the German reformer.

Of those Lutherans who have written extensively on Luther during the last few decades, one of the most important is Gerhard Ritter, author of the next selection. He stresses Luther's own religious experience as the key to the meaning of the German Reformation. It was the renewal of the spiritual life of the Middle Ages in Luther himself and in the lives of his followers that made the Reformation a specifically German spiritual revival. For this reason one must understand Luther not only as a Christian but particularly as a German-Christian. Was Luther as significant as Ritter believes?

Perhaps an answer to this question is provided by E. G. Schwiebert who, in the selection from his biography of Luther, attempts to give the setting of the reformer's work, and in so doing seeks to indicate his true importance. He feels that the social situation in which Luther carried on his reforming activities furnishes no simple explanation, for although Luther undoubtedly held a dominant position, he was aided by two forces; the university and the printing press, without which his views could not have attained widespread circulation. Is this view unduly circumscribed? Did not Luther's army include sailors, merchants, and professional men who carried his views throughout Germany and Europe? Indeed, from what Schwiebert himself says, may one not conclude that Luther was the product rather than the molder of the forces around him?

Although the Lutheran and the Reformed interpretations of the Reformation have for a long time dominated Protestant historiography, another point of view put forward frequently today emphasizes the place of the "radical" reformers, the Anabaptists. Norman Cohn in *The Pursuit of the Millennium* has shown something of the background of this radical, lower-class movement in the Middle Ages, while Roland H. Bainton in *The Reformation of the Sixteenth Century* and other writings has constantly stressed the Anabaptists' importance. Some of their advocates go so far as to say that they were the true Protestant reformers, for they alone went the whole way.

One of the most significant works on this aspect of the Reformation to appear recently is that of George Hunston Williams who in *The Radical Reformation*, from which a selection is reprinted here, seeks to provide a perspective on the Reformation which gives the Anabaptists full credit. As Williams points out, however, the reformers such as Luther, Zwingli, and Calvin opposed these Protestants vigorously, and one cannot but wonder if the Anabaptists should really be regarded as part of the Reformation and not as an entirely separate movement. It may be that they are now regarded as Protestants only because their descendants, for example the Baptists, later aligned themselves with the Protestants. If this be the case, should they even be considered in a study of the Reformation?

Although the Protestants have usually stressed the role of individual leaders and the specifically doctrinal issues, in recent years some Protestant historians, particularly those in the United States, have sought to give an account of the Reformation with due regard for the various religious, economic, social, and political forces involved. They still give credit to leaders such as Luther and Calvin, but they try to see them in their environments and to understand the various influences that helped to mold not only a few individuals but the movement as a whole. Kenneth Scott Latourette of Yale has employed this synthetic approach in his *History of Christianity*, and Roland H. Bainton employs the same perspective in a short introduction to a collection of documents on the Reformation, from which the next selection is taken. This is now the more typical American view of the Reformation.

Bainton's should be compared with the approach of the other Protestant writers in order to evaluate their relative usefulness and to see how the Protestant understanding of the movement has developed over the past century.

Since the days of the Reformation, most Roman Catholics have regarded it with alarm and intense dislike. Not only did the sixteenth-century ecclesiastics charged with refuting the claims of Luther, Zwingli, Calvin, and the others condemn the reformers roundly, but the Council of Trent (1543–1564) anathematized their views and Roman Catholic writers in the following years kept up the barrage. Early in the reign of Louis XIV of France, Louis Maimbourg published a four-volume work, two volumes recounting the evil history of Lutheranism and two the equally bad, if not worse, history of Calvinism. A few years later Bishop Jacques-Bénigne Bossuet made a further historical attack in his *Histoire des Variations des Églises Protestantes* (1688). Such attitudes toward the Reformation were, however, by no means limited to France or to the seventeenth century.

That such an outlook on the Reformation continued into the nineteenth century is evidenced by writers such as the Germans Johann Döllinger, Johannes Janssen, and Ludwig von Pastor. No one, however, expressed his antagonism to the Protestant account of the movement more clearly or forcefully than Martin J. Spalding when, as Bishop of Louisville, he wrote *The History of the Protestant Reformation* (1860) in reply to the work of Merle d'Aubigné. In two volumes he sought to disprove practically everything the Protestant writer had said. In the selection from this work included here he deals particularly with Merle d'Aubigné's philosophy of the Reformation. It would seem that Spalding regards the movement more as a *de*-formation than a *re*-formation and the Protestant historian as, to put it mildly, somewhat biased. Might one not conclude that Spalding, too, has his particular axe to grind? What, for instance, is his explanation of the success and failure of the movement in different parts of Europe?

In more recent years, Roman Catholic apologists and critics have tended to follow somewhat different approaches to the Reformation. For them, as for many Protestants, the personality of Luther has become an important subject of study. P. H. Grisar, S.J., in *Martin Luther, His Life and Work* (1960) has sought to explain Luther's ideas and actions largely on psychological grounds. In the excerpt reprinted here he presents the background of the Reformation in Germany. A comparison of his description with those of Ritter and Schwiebert will point up the difference between the Protestant and Roman Catholic views of Luther. Is there any real divergence of thought on this subject?

While Grisar stresses the importance of Luther's ideas, others feel that the motivations of whole groups, not of one individual, were of greater significance.

To many Roman Catholics, the motivation of most Protestants was greed, the desire to acquire the Church's lands. Such an analysis of the Reformation of course rejects most Protestant views and tends to align itself with the Marxist approach, a juxtaposition that is, to say the least, anomalous. Nevertheless, Hugh Ross Williamson in the selection from *The Beginnings of the English Reformation* (1957) feels that this view provides the only proper understandings of the English Reformation, and one cannot but wonder why he does not apply it fully to what happened also on the Continent. It is only fair to point out that many of Williamson's fellow Roman Catholics who have written, on this subject, among them Father Philip Hughes and G. A. T. O'Brien, have not adopted the same point of view.

The views of Grisar and Williamson are characteristic of the 1920s when much emphasis was laid upon sociological and economic forces in history. Since World War II, attitudes have begun to change, partly as a result of the spread of Communism and partly because of the growing influence of ecumenicalism fostered by the World Council of Churches and by some of the popes, especially John XXIII and Paul VI. In accordance with this new attitude, many Roman Catholic historians have tended to become somewhat more conciliatory and even sympathetic in their accounts of the Reformation. Among these is Georges Tavard who has written a number of works on Protestant–Roman Catholic relations and a small volume devoted entirely to Protestantism. In the latter work, from which a selection is included here, he presents an analysis of the fundamental doctrines of the Reformation and seeks to show that there is no ineradicable difference between them and Catholic beliefs. How far would Protestants accept this idea? And what do other Roman Catholics think of it?

A Roman Catholic view somewhat different, although supplementary to the primarily theological explanations of the Reformation, comes from the Roman Catholic historians who seek answers in the general condition of the Church. Although they in no way accept the Protestants' claims that the Church had corrupted true Christian doctrine, lacked spiritual life, or was irreformably immoral, they believe that the state of the church in the sixteenth century was such that it may have given this impression and that as a result a revolt could have been expected. The two leading exponents of this view have been Joseph Lortz of the Institute for European History in Mainz and P. Janelle of the Université de Clermont. In Janelle's analysis of the state of the Church, the next selection, one finds much that recalls some of the Protestant views, but he does not draw the conclusions of Luther, Calvin or the modern Protestant historians. The question is, why not? Is it because he and the Protestant historians differ in their primary assumptions? Moreover, does he really provide any explanation as to why the Reformation took place?

The Roman Catholic interpretation of the Protestant Reformation, like the Protestant interpretation, has developed and changed over the past century or more. One must still ask: What is the Roman Catholic explanation of the Reformation? The Protestants have held that it was ultimately a spiritual revival which, as Merle d'Aubigné has said, manifested the action of God in history. Do the Roman Catholic interpreters in fact reject Spalding's position, or have they merely become a little more sophisticated in the statement of their case?

Although historians interested in the Reformation have usually approached the subject from either the Protestant or the Roman Catholic point of view, some adherents of the latter, as we have seen, sought to explain the movement on economic or social grounds. This orientation is more typical, however, of historians with a primarily secular approach. While these have shown an appreciation of the Reformation's importance, they regard it as a socio-historical phenomenon rather than as an ultimately religious movement. They have thought of the religious dynamic of the Reformation as socially generated.

Such an understanding is present in Preserved Smith's *The Age of the Reformation* (1920), from which a selection is reprinted here. He holds that the religious revolution involved in the rise of Protestantism resulted from contemporary changes in scientific knowledge and ethical feeling. The new doctrines expressed the same attitudes as did the new nationalism, capitalism, and individualism in other spheres of life. Consequently, the Reformation in Smith's thinking possesses a character very different from that attributed to it by Protestants or Roman Catholics. But was there truly a Reformation if this explanation is correct? What are Smith's basic assumptions? How does he relate his assumed causes to the movement itself?

As an advocate of the socio-economic determination of history, Eva Priester of Austria approaches the problem from another angle, as seen in the next selection. Apparently accepting the dictum of Marx's friend Friedrich Engels "that the determining element in history is *ultimately* production and reproduction in real life," she seeks to explain the Reformation on socio-economic grounds. Completely ignoring the religious dimension of the movement, she presents an explanation that she feels is scientific and objective. While her emphasis is a necessary corrective to much writing on the Reformation, does she give a more accurate picture of the Reformation than do those who emphasize the religious issues?

Up to this point none of the selections presented has dealt with the influence of the Renaissance on the Reformation, particularly with the question of whether the religious movement was merely a northern extension of the literary and artistic revival in Italy. The relationship of the two has been a matter of discussion for many years, and various views have been advanced from Theodore Beza's *Histoire Ecclésiastique* (1580) to Hiram Haydn's

Counter-Renaissance (1950). The selection from H. A. E. van Gelder offers a somewhat unusual perspective, although it is related to Haydn's concept as indicated in the title of his work. Van Gelder claims that the real Reformation was established not by Luther, Zwingli, Calvin, and their followers but by those who carried on the humanist tradition of the Renaissance, which eventually came to full expression in the Enlightenment of the seventeenth and eighteenth centuries. What then is the essential nature of the movement commonly known as the Protestant Reformation? Van Gelder seems to place the Reformation in a category completely different from that of the other writers. For this he has been criticized severely by some historians, but may it not be that he has done what others have failed to do? Has he not brought out the radical conflict between the principles of the Renaissance and of the Reformation, which may be necessary for an understanding of both movements?

In view of the divergent interpretations of the Reformation, we should remind ourselves, at the end of this study, of the need to strive constantly for objectivity. In the last selection Peter Masten Dunne, S.J., makes a plea for impartiality, yet he also points out some of the difficulties in attaining it. His article raises the question as to whether any historian can have a completely detached attitude toward the Reformation. Will not the Reformation remain a matter of discussion and controversy as long as historians have presuppositions, religious or otherwise, that influence their views and reactions?

How objective are historians when dealing with the Reformation? Perhaps these selections from different historians, with their various and often conflicting points of view, leave the student with the feeling that he can never really understand the movement. This undoubtedly is true unless he can acquire a suprahistorical position free from his own environment. He must, however, taking all mundane interpretations into account seek the truth, with the constant realization that any explanation can only be approximate.

In the reprinted selections footnotes appearing in the original sources have in general been omitted unless they contribute to the argument or better understanding of the selection.

The historian who more than any other established the Protestant interpretation of the Reformation in Protestant Europe and throughout the English-speaking world was JEAN HENRI MERLE D'AUBIGNÉ (1794–1872). One of the leaders of the Evangelical Church in Switzerland, he devoted his life to the task of writing an exhaustive history of the Reformation, the first volume appearing in 1835 and the thirteenth and last after his death. Translated into many languages, his work provided the interpretation which for many Protestants is still the standard, as is indicated by a recent reprinting of the portion of his work dealing with the Reformation in England.*

▶ # God's Action in History

The work I have undertaken is not the history of a party. It is the history of one of the greatest revolutions ever effected in human affairs—the history of a mighty impulse communicated to the world three centuries ago—and of which the operation is still everywhere discernible in our own days. The history of the Reformation is altogether distinct from the history of Protestantism. In the former all bears the character of a regeneration of human nature, a religious and social transformation emanating from God himself. In the latter, we see too often a glaring depravation of first principles—the conflict of parties—a sectarian spirit—and the operation of private interests. The history of Protestantism might claim the attention only of Protestants. The history of the Reformation is a book for all Christians—or rather for all mankind.

An historian may choose his portion in the field before him. He may narrate the great events which change the exterior aspect of a nation, or of the world; or he may record that tranquil progression of a nation, of the church, or of mankind, which generally follows mighty changes in social relations. Both these departments of history are of high importance. But the public interest has seemed to turn, by preference, to those periods which, under the name of Revo-

* Reprinted from Jean Henri Merle d'Aubigné, *History of the Great Reformation of the Sixteenth Century* (New York, 1846), vol. I, pp. iii–v.

lutions, bring forth a nation, or society at large for a new era—and to a new career.

Of the last kind is the transformation which, with very feeble powers, I have attempted to describe, in the hope that the beauty of the subject will compensate for my insufficiency. The name of *revolution* which I here give to it, is, in our days, brought into discredit with many who almost confound it with revolt. But this is to mistake its meaning. A revolution is a change wrought in human affairs. It is a something new which unrolls itself from the bosom of humanity; and the word, previously to the close of the last century, was more frequently understood in a good sense, than in a bad one: "a happy—a wonderful Revolution" was the expression. The Reformation, being the re-establishment of the principles of primitive Christianity, was the reverse of a revolt. It was a movement *regenerative* of that which was destined to revive; but *conservative* of that which is to stand for ever. Christianity and the Reformation, while they established the great principle of the equality of souls in the sight of God, and overturned the usurpations of a proud priesthood which assumed to place itself between the Creator and his creature, at the same time laid down as a first element of social order, that there is no power but what is of God—and called on all men to love the brethren, to fear God, to honour the king.

The Reformation is entirely distinguished from the revolutions of antiquity, and from the greater part of those of modern times. In these, the question is one of politics, and the object proposed is the establishment or overthrow of the power of the one, or of the many. The love of truth, of holiness, of eternal things, was the simple and powerful spring which gave effect to that which we have to narrate. It is the evidence of a gradual advance in human nature. In truth, if man, instead of seeking only material, temporal, and earthly interests, aims at a higher object and seeks spiritual and immortal blessings—he advances, he progresses. The Reformation is one of the most memorable days of this progress. It is a pledge that the struggle of our own times will terminate in favour of truth, by a triumph yet more spiritual and glorious.

Christianity and the Reformation are two of the greatest revolutions in history. They were not limited to one nation, like the various political movements which history records, but extented to many nations, and their effects are destined to be felt to the ends of the earth.

Christianity and the Reformation are, indeed, the same revolution, but working at different periods, and in dissimilar circumstances. They differ in secondary features: they are alike in their first lines and leading characteristics. The one is the re-appearance of the other. The former closes the old order of things; the latter begins the new. Between them is the middle age. One is the parent of the other; and if the daughter is, in some respects, inferior, she has, in others, characters altogether peculiar to herself.

The suddenness of its action is one of these characters of the Reformation. The great revolutions which have drawn after them the fall of a monarchy, or an entire change of political system, or launched the human mind in a new career of development, have been slowly and gradually prepared; the power to be displaced has long been mined, and its principal supports have given way. It was even thus at the introduction of Christianity. But the Reformation, at the first glance, seems to offer a different aspect. The Church of Rome is seen, under Leo X., in all its strength and glory. A monk speaks—and in the half of Europe this power and glory suddenly crumble into dust. This revolution reminds us of the words by which the Son of God announces his second advent: "As the lightning cometh forth from the west and shineth unto the east, so shall also the coming of the Son of man be."

This rapidity is inexplicable to those who see in this great event only a reform; who make it simply an act of critical judgment, consisting in a choice of doctrines,—the abandoning of some, the preserving others, and combining those retained, so as to make of them a new code of doctrine.

How could an entire people?—how could many nations have so rapidly performed so difficult a work? How could such an act of critical judgment kindle the enthusiasm indispensable to great and especially to sudden revolutions? But the Reformation was an event of a very different kind; and this its history will prove. It was the pouring forth anew of that life which Christianity had brought into the world. It was the triumph of the noblest of doctrines—of that which animates those who receive it with the purest and most powerful enthusiasm—the doctrine of *Faith*—the doctrine of *Grace*. If the Reformation had been what many Catholics and Protestants imagine—if it had been that negative system of a negative reason, which rejects with childish impatience whatever displeases it, and disowns the grand ideas and leading truths of universal Christianity—it would never have overpassed the threshold of an academy —of a cloister, or even of a monk's cell. But it had no sympathy with what is commonly intended by the word Protestantism. Far from having sustained any

loss of vital energy, it arose at once like a man full of strength and resolution.

Two considerations will account for the rapidity and extent of this revolution. One of these must be sought in God, the other among men. The impulse was given by an unseen hand of power, and the change which took place was the work of God. This will be the conclusion arrived at by every one who considers the subject with impartiality and attention, and does not rest in a superficial view. But the historian has a further office to perform:—God acts by second causes. Many circumstances, which have often escaped observation, gradually prepared men for the great transformation of the sixteenth century, so that the human mind was ripe when the hour of its emancipation arrived.

The office of the historian is to combine these two principal elements in the picture he presents. This is what is attempted in the present work. We shall be easily understood, so long as we investigate the secondary causes which contributed to bring about the revolution we have undertaken to describe. Many will, perhaps, be slower of comprehension, and will be inclined even to charge us with superstition, when we shall ascribe to God the accomplishment of the work. And yet that thought is what we particularly cherish. The history takes as its guiding star the simple and pregnant truth that God is in History. But this truth is commonly forgotten, and sometimes disputed. It seems fit, therefore, that we should open our views, and by so doing justify the course we have taken.

In these days, history can no longer be that dead letter of facts to recording which the majority of the earlier historians confined themselves. It is felt that, as in man's nature, so in his history, there are two elements—matter and spirit. Our great writers, unwilling to restrict themselves to the production of a simple recital, which would have been but a barren chronicle, have sought for some principle of life to animate the materials of the past.

Some have borrowed such a principle from the rules of art; they have aimed at the simplicity, truth, and *picturesque* of description; and have endeavoured to make their narratives *live* by the interest of the events themselves.

Others have sought in philosophy the spirit which should fecundate their labours. With incidents they have intermingled reflections—instruction—political and philosophic truths—and have thus enlivened their recitals with a moral which they have elicited from them, or ideas they have been able to associate with them.

Both these methods are, doubtless, useful, and should be employed within certain limits. But there is another source whence we must above all seek for the ability to enter into the understanding, the mind, and the life of past ages;—and this is religion. History must live by that principle of life which is proper to it, and that life is God. He must be acknowledged and proclaimed in history;—and the course of events must be displayed as the annals of the government of a Supreme Disposer.

E. G. LÈONARD (1891–1961) at the time of his death occupied the chair of the Reformation and Protestantism in the École Pratique des Hautes Études (Sorbonne). One of the leading Protestant historians of France, he was for a time the manuscript librarian of the Bibliothèque Nationale in Paris, and taught in Naples, Italy, and Caen and Aix in France. His numerous writings have received wide recognition, but the most important work is his *Histoire Generale du Protestantisme* (1963), from which the present selection is taken.*

Revival of the Church's Life

The path of Reformation history is strewn with meaningless questions and meaningless answers; let us begin by clearing the ground.

There is the meaningless question of the inevitability of the religious revolution of the sixteenth century and of the schism which ensued. One may, naturally, regret that they happened, but it is idle to deny the authenticity of the fact. Again, to regard the Reformation solely as the outcome of a tragic misunderstanding, of the temporary failure of the Catholic Church and the culpable haste of the Reformers, is to confine it unduly to the sixteenth century: we

are now in the twentieth century; the spiritual contingencies are quite different, but the Reformation—I do not say Protestantism—continues; its reasons were not dictated by time and place.

There is the meaningless question of its national, or geographical, origins, and of the direction in which it was diffused. The fact is that Luther appeared in Germany; but three years after the Theses there were "Lutherans" all over Europe. When a problem of vital importance concerns a whole world, and it adopts, from the first and everywhere at once, the solution found in a particular place, this place itself is of little account.

* Reprinted from E. G. Lèonard, *History of Protestantism* (London: Thomas Nelson & Sons, Ltd., 1966), vol. I, pp. 1–5. This work was originally published as *Histoire Generale du Protestantisme* (Paris: Presses Universitaires, 1963). Footnotes omitted.

13

In a forest fire, the match, or the fragment of glass, which set light to the first twigs is a trifle compared with the dryness of the pines, oozing with resin under a scorching sun. Then there is the direction in which the Reformation spread! From east to west, say the authorities, and London, Geneva and Amsterdam are, indeed, to the west of Wittenberg. But what of Hungary? It is true that Bas-Poitou was affected before Saintonge and helped to evangelise the latter through a nobleman of the time, M. de Pons; but the beautifully straight east-west line which could thus be drawn would have to pass through Italy, since it was in Ferrara, at the court of Renée of France, that M. de Pons was won over by Calvin. The wind may sometimes spread the fire in a certain direction, but the forester must also take account of back-eddies of flames, of sparks scattered afar and of spontaneous combustion in the over-heated atmosphere.

We will not class among the meaningless questions raised by the appearance of the Reformation that of its explanation. But though we may legitimately seek for one, we must beware of meaningless answers, even when they can claim to have won wide acceptance, sometimes for centuries past. We have, moreover, been set upon the right path by the now classic article by Lucien Febvre: "Les origines de la Réforme française et le problème des causes générales de la Réforme", *Revue historique*, CLXI (1929), pp. 1–73. Let us follow it, and carry it a little further.

The *moral explanation* of the Reformation has long been that favoured by the Catholics. Adopting the traditional position of the anti-Protestant polemists, M. Maritain can still write, on the subject of Luther: "This, if I may say so, is no more than the classic story of the fallen monk." But the Protestants long maintained, and still do occasionally, that the Reformation was a reaction against the licentiousness of the priests and the debaucheries of the Papacy; they are confirmed in this view by a late writing in which Luther claims that his revolt arose from his horrified discovery of the shameful practices of Rome, during his visit to Italy.

Catholics and Protestants agree in supplementing this moral explanation with a *political explanation*, to account for the spread of the Reformation. The former have traditionally attributed this to the covetousness of the princes and nobility, thirsting to despoil the Church. But the latter accepted this statement of the position when, for example, they chose to attribute the failure of the Reformation in France primarily to the opposition of Francis I, freed from such temptation by the Concordat of 1516.

According to a more recent *economic and social explanation*, favoured by the agnostic school, the history of the Reformation should give virtual pride of place to considerations directly concerned with the aspirations and material needs of the different classes. Karl Marx —for whom religions were "the children of their time" and "the children of the economy, that universal mother of human societies"—already regarded "the Reformation, the great and powerful Reformation which was born in the sixteenth century" as "the child of that new form of economy which arose at this time, imposed itself upon the world and rapidly conquered it—the capitalist economy." Henri Hauser, moderate and discriminating, in an epoch-making article published many years ago, was content to suggest a blend of the material and the spiritual: "The Reformation of the sixteenth century has the dual character of a social revolution and a religious revolution." More recently one of the Italian adherents of historical materialism, Corrado Barbagallo, declared that "the Reformation did not stem from religious causes, nor from a more exact and faithful interpretation of Christian truth." He even wrote: "I could not credit the conclusion that great multitudes, in this or that country, could really have been interested in the theological subtleties of a Luther, a Zwingli, a Melanchthon, or an Oecolampadius, which were scarcely understood by professional theologians. . . . I have therefore regarded the Reformation not as a predominantly religious phenomenon, but as the religious expression, aspect and disguise of the crisis experienced by every country in Europe during the second half of the sixteenth century."

Other historians have concentrated rather on the regions where the Reformation prospered, and have attempted *geographical and psychological explanations* of its destiny. Noting its appearance along the great highways, some see it as the fruit of itinerant preaching and colportage, and so give a predominant place in its history to the activity of the propagandists. Others, on the contrary, turning their attention to the mental climate of the communities and countries affected, and finding them at other times receptive to movements of political and social resistance (Chouannerie, Socialism, etc.), are inclined to see in their religious attitude the manifestation of a non-conformist temperament.

One is conscious of a specious and tendentious element in all these explanations. On the question of morality, modern Catholic historiography has, in general, given up seeking the cause of the Reformation in the immorality of licentious monks. Lucien Febvre invites Protestant historians to make a similar correction: the attempts to reform discipline in the preceding period had already borne fruit; moreover, the Reformers attached much less blame to the morals of the clergy than had their precursors of the fourteenth and fifteenth centuries. The argument concerning the material interests of the princes and nobility who decided for or against the Reformation ignores the fact that they, too, had souls and minds alive to spiritual problems and that, when these interests indicated profitable conversion, they remained, more often than not, faithful to their existing position. As to the economic and social explanation, let us observe only—without denying the primary importance of material things in the destiny of mankind, or agreeing with Croce that the basis of history is ethical and not economic—that the motives invoked by this explanation apply so widely to the whole of early sixteenth-century society, whether receptive or resistant to the new ideas, that they cease to be determining factors: if, as will be shown, the Reformation appeared at one and the same time among both rich and poor, both in the towns and in the countryside, then it did not primarily derive from economic and social situations. To lay too exclusive a stress on geography and the natural channels for propagation is to minimise unduly, to the advantage of the activity of the preachers and the colporteurs, the part played by the inclinations of the people among whom they were working; moreover, the Reformation very quickly appeared in places far from the great highways (in France, for example, Brittany and

Béarn) and, everywhere, the very great results obtained by the small number of propagandists oblige us to take account, above all, of the souls they evangelised. But should we also take account of the different temperaments they encountered? This would be to solve one problem by raising another, even vaster and more difficult—the relation between faith, the soul and particular temperaments.

To sum up: if, in tracing the causes of the Reformation, we eliminate those which apply only to one particular class or region and establish the fact that it affected all countries and men in every walk of life, we must then recognise that it had causes which were valid for all mankind. None of these general causes is more universal than religious feeling. It is, in any case, natural enough to look for specifically religious reasons for a religious revolution. But, as we have seen, until the vigorous reaction of Lucien Febvre, many historians scarcely realised the fact.

The Protestants, it is true, had understood. But just as they missed the real solution of the problem by attaching undue importance to the moral weaknesses of the Catholic clergy, they very often went astray even when they laid the emphasis on faith. Indeed, they give us the impression that the Reformation was a reaction against a Catholic Church in which spirituality had grown progressively more parched, and farther removed from the Bible and the Saviour. I must emphasise at the outset—for it is one of the basic principles and guiding themes of this book—that *the Reformation, far more than a revolt against Catholic faith, was its culmination and its full flowering.*

The reader will learn the reasons which lead me to this conclusion, and the nature of the domestic crisis which caused the Reformation to take place outside the traditional Church, instead of being its second internal reform (the first being that of Gregory VII and St Bernard). He will also see the way in which, since then, the gulf has only grown wider, so that the periodic attempts to narrow it have increasingly taken on the appearance of illusions or manoeuvres, ever more certain to fail. As the emancipated child of the Catholic Church, Protestantism has assumed, for a great body of Christians, the task once incumbent on its parent. It is thereby required to repeat her experiments, and often to confirm her findings. In many cases, it has re-encountered the problems which had faced the old Church since the end of the ancient world. And though Protestantism itself, as a whole, is now four hundred years old, each of its subsidiary "denominations" and bodies finds the same problems and often their Catholic solutions. But it is not only the successor of Catholicism. During the four centuries of their co-existence, the two cults have been confronted, at any given moment, by the same questions, for the spiritual attitudes of men, whether of the one or the other obedience, cannot be very different in the face of circumstances common to a whole nation, or a whole continent. Western Catholicism and Protestantism experienced the same decline in the eighteenth century; the Protestant Revival in Europe, from 1815 to 1830, was the exact counterpart of the Catholic renaissance during the French Restoration; a more recent period has seen Catholicism and Protestantism equally at grips with oppression.

They have encountered similar problems, successively or at the same time; they have suffered trials in common— that in itself ensures that this study, in which Protestantism is, I trust, presented in all its fidelity, greatness and fundamental unity, will be the history not of a schism, but of the Church.

While Merle d'Aubigné and Lèonard wrote about the Reformation from a Reformed, or Calvinist, point of view, GERHARD RITTER (b. 1888) writes with a Lutheran perspective. As a German Lutheran who has held important academic positions in Munich, Leipzig, Heidelberg, and Berlin, Ritter wrote with authority when he produced his work in the early 1920s. Although previous German Lutheran writers had emphasized Luther's place in the Reformation, Ritter sought to bring it into even sharper focus by stressing his character as a German. In so doing, Ritter may also reflect the rising German nationalism that was beginning to reassert itself in the wake of World War I.*

Luther's Place in the Reformation

But the battle-cry of the warrior was not Martin Luther's last word to the German people. If we look for the enduring and positive results of his life and particularly for what he has to say to us, then we must turn back to the reflections with which we began our study. The most general and permanent achievement of his life lies in his own personal secret: in his life with God and in the direct relationship of all his thinking and willing with him—in this particular respect, that with Luther everything which is external springs as it were automatically from a faith which bursts the bonds of the human imagination.

It is in his simple religious insights that we find the true meaning of the man. The key to his ethics is his proclamation of the supremacy of the eternal, the law of God, over all human action, and his consequent rejection of ecclesiastical authority or of any considerations of man's own happiness. He strove constantly to establish the idea of man's direct, personal and inescapable responsibility to God firmly in men's consciousness until it completely dominated men's lives, so that they might experience again the release from the intolerable tensions which had been set up by casuistry and teleological ethics.

* From: *Luther: His Life and Work* by Gerhard Ritter. Copyright © 1959 by F. Bruckmann K. G. Verlag., Munchen. Copyright © 1963 in English Translation by William Collins Sons & Co., Ltd., London, and Harper & Row, Inc., New York. Reprinted by permission of Harper & Row. Introduction and pp. 210–217. Footnotes omitted.

He gave men a new vision of the exaltation of the human self, regardless of its limitations, of an exaltation which can only be experienced as a gift from God and which man can neither bring to pass nor truly understand. Just as a flame, once it has been lit, will warm and illuminate everything which comes close to it, so the true attitude of the heart in which eternal life beats strongly will transform and ennoble all outward action as it were automatically. It was this vision which inspired all his teaching on individual and social action. The development of this religious message was the true fruit of his literary work, and it owed its power to the fact that Luther's message did not derive from any personal opinion, but from the depths of his fundamental religious experience: from an experience which was indeed of a highly personal nature, but which was intended in no way to be individual, original or in any sense new, but rather a reliving, a faithful acceptance of the earliest Christian revelation. The West has indeed produced in plenty saints and founders of religious orders and of new ideals of piety and of new religious communities (from the Church Fathers to the days of the Pietists and beyond), in whom the purity of the religious impulse was certainly no less genuine than it was in the case of Martin Luther. Nor has it been lacking in reformers before, since or even then; bold men of great determination who were genuinely grieved by the ruins of the worldly Church grown cold in the grip of its hierarchy, and who created new forms of spiritual life—in part with more skill and outward success than the monk from Wittenberg. But not one of these penetrated so deeply into the heart of the message of primitive Christianity as he, and no one before had been able

to transform Christian life so completely from within. So no one has as much right to the title of the renovator of Western Christianity as has Martin Luther. He, and no other, stands at the end of an age which is passing away, and at the beginning of a new religious epoch.

This is of infinitely greater significance than his negative achievements, infinitely greater than the destruction of the universal dominion of the Papacy. For this was only partially successful in spite of the misery which was inflicted on European humanity by a century of religious wars, in spite of the irreparable split in the German nation which must (though this is only partly justified) be laid to his charge. Since then the Roman Catholic Church has shown a thousand times over that her power to come to the aid of men was by no means exhausted but merely slumbering. Admittedly, it required a man like Luther to rouse it by his attack and this is not the least of his historical achievements; but even many Protestants would be inclined to admit that the political form of Christian community which is the essence of the Catholic hierarchy and which Luther was so eager to destroy, does still have its particular, if limited, value in the world of today alongside the free preaching of the Word. Should we applaud the chorus of those Rationalists and religious neutrals who since the sixteenth century have seen the real achievement of our hero in the destruction of the "medieval outlook" (by which they understand nothing but Christian dogma in its scholastic expression, which is then censored as "dark" and mysterious); indeed in an (unconscious) victory over the Christian concept of God, according to the most recent discoveries? Whoever approaches him from this side will always be disappointed by him; for he did not destroy the world of ideas of the Middle Ages as a whole but the Rationalism of a much later age whose first modest forerunners in Erasmus, the enthusiasts and "sacramentalisers," he persecuted with all the bitter hatred of a medieval heresy-hunter (although admittedly without his sword and fire). He transformed, purified, deepened and renewed the thought and sensitivity of the Middle Ages but he did not abolish them; it was others who came after him who undermined and destroyed them. Or should we fête him above all as the founder of Protestant church order? Our study has already shown over and over again how little we would touch the core of his being in this, how little we would show the ultimate significance of his work. His achievement would appear scanty beside that of the other reformers. For it was just the Lutheran state church which was always the weakest and most insignificant of all; it has never (except in Sweden) thrown off the traces of the oppressed and miserable world of the small German states in which it grew up. But just as Luther's weakness as an organiser was inseparably bound up with his greatest qualities, so it was with the Protestant churches. Even if their earthly appearance bears something of the character of a temporary structure, this appears to be the inevitable complement to its radical rejection of any claim to worldly power, which is an essential part of its character. No, the foundation of the German state church is by no means adequate to convey the significance of his historical achievement. Way above all confessional, ecclesiastical and national limitations, his religious message, in which we find the true fruits of his life's work, spread its influence for the re-

moulding of Western culture in all the great ferment of the sixteenth century. The world-wide effect of the Reformation far surpasses the spiritual horizon of even its founder himself. Without at first suspecting it and without later realising the extent of its possibilities, he had by his action helped to determine the spirit of a new epoch in history.

It is (or at any rate was) a widely accepted error to consider his work, the Reformation, as a part of a more general phenomenon, which we usually call the Renaissance of the West—that great spiritual movement which destroyed the veil, "woven out of faith, prejudice and fancy," which lay on the "dreaming, half-sleeping" minds of the Middle Ages (Burckhardt). However, the German Reformation was not merely part of the Renaissance, nor even a parallel phenomenon, but to a much greater extent it was its counterpart. It trundled along like an enormous block of stone flowing from the Middle Ages to the general secularisation of thought and sensitivity of the modern age. It was in fact the most powerful restraining influence on the tendency to distort and to sweep away the spirit of Christianity. It was Luther's real historical role to rekindle this spirit, this most valuable inheritance of the Middle Ages, and so to make it fruitful for the future history of Western civilisation. Even the rekindling of medieval piety which shortly afterwards began to spread across the whole of the West from Spain in the age of the Catholic Counter-Reformation would not have achieved its universal importance without his action. The old Church had first to be shaken to its very foundations by the falling away of the Germanic peoples, before the way was made clear for the spirits which even there had long been active under the cover of the hierarchical tradition. Renaissance, Reformation and Catholic Restoration—these were from now on the three great spiritual forces whose conflict gave birth to the modern world, by whose tensions the spirit of the modern national cultures was everywhere, and everywhere quite differently, determined.

Yet, if we should seek to calculate the significance of the spiritual heritage of Luther as an active agent in this process of development and ferment, or to discover the ways by which ideas and tendencies of Lutheran origin have continued to bear influence on the many ramifications of modern culture within Germany and far beyond its borders, and with what success, then we shall find ourselves dealing with highly controversial questions, towards whose serious solution only the very first tentative steps have been taken. Our chief concern is to approach the question from the side which is easiest of access for us as Germans; we shall be able to see Martin Luther's importance for the world most easily reflected in our own example; indeed it was in Germany that his work came nearest to having its desired effect; and it is surely true that in his whole manner and character he is far more easily accessible and familiar to us than to other peoples, simply because we can feel that he belongs to us as a German. There was a time when our young students used to fête him with overwhelming enthusiasm as a "German hero," as the ideal of German manhood—those youths who went off to fight in the war of liberation against Napoleon and who returned home with high ideals of a new, free, unified, but also devout, Germany, liberated from the false faith of the

Italians. Today we have moved far from the excesses of early German nationalism; yet why should this prevent us from recognising certain characteristic traits of the German national character with its strength, its weaknesses and dangers, in Martin Luther?

It is only since the time of the Reformation that German spiritual life has begun to assume certain clearly recognisable traits of its own. The medieval man and Christian, as we saw, was always in a certain sense a European. It was the age of the religious wars which first gave the modern nations their sharply defined characteristics, and it is one of the most tragic facts of German history that the nation should have been split in two by the confessional struggle. Yet German Rationalism and German Idealism both attempted to tone down the differences and to do away with them. Who would deny that they have extensively influenced the spiritual disposition of even the Catholic part of our nation? And who would deny that their spiritual home was in Protestant Germany? So it is not in the least to disregard our Catholic fellow-countrymen if we attempt to understand ourselves in the light of Martin Luther's character. We will be concerned with very natural things. In what form and pattern did he bring up his people? For centuries every family in Protestant Germany went daily or at least every Sunday to church, where the deep and rich thoughts of the Reformer, which were offered in his book of sermons, were preached from the pulpit either in his original words or else in a thousand attenuated and varied forms. There they sang his vigorous tunes and the heroic verses of his hymns, from which the German people has from generation to generation in its recurring tribulations drawn new comfort and courage to hope and to stand fast:

And should it last throughout the night
And still be there at daybreak,
Yet will my heart in God's great might
Its courage ever take.

Then, not infrequently, the head of the family would question the children and the servants on the Little Catechism: "that the old Adam in us should, by daily remorse and penance, be drowned and should die with all his sins and evil lusts." Finally, in every house there was Luther's Bible, whose sayings, in his deeply poetic translation, became a real part of our national heritage, and whose incomparably sonorous tones are re-echoed in the language of our greatest poets; and none of its books had more impact than the one which is translated in the most typically Lutheran way, the Psalms, in whose trembling and yet heroic trust in God he found his own spiritual life most truly reflected (and it is surely no mere chance that his academic lectures on the Bible dealt with this book remarkably frequently!). "Whither shall I go from thy spirit and whither shall I flee from thy presence? If I ascend up into heaven thou art there: if I make my bed in hell, behold thou art there also. If I take the wings of the morning and dwell in the uttermost parts of the sea, even there shall thy hand lead me and thy right hand shall hold me." Could it be otherwise than that this enormous educational programme which was undertaken by the new Church and which extended into every sphere of daily life and work, illuminating them in the light of moral considerations, should have gradually been infused into the blood of the whole nation and have become a permanent leavening in its nature? The more the mere presentation of the sacramental means of grace retreated in the Lutheran Church, by contrast with the medieval Church, behind the infinite and the religious and moral claim on every individual, the more intensive became its spiritual effect. Luther himself was at times surprised at the new spirit of the youth, which was growing up under his eyes. Of course, he was as unable to leave behind a fully competent heir to his spirit, as was any other of the great men of our people: but however little his followers may have understood the true and genuine Luther with their strict orthodoxy, and however certainly it involved a serious relapse into the theological scholasticism of the late Middle Ages—even in the miserable form of this orthodox Lutheranism there still lived on enough of his spirit, to carry on his work as he would have wished.

What may be termed an American approach to the subject of Luther's place in the Reformation appears in the work of E. G. SCHWIEBERT (b. 1895). After graduate work at Ohio State and Chicago universities, he received his Ph.D. from Cornell University in 1930. He has taught at a number of American universities and also at the University of Erlangen, Germany. He was cofounder and first president of the American Society for Reformation Research and executive director of the Foundation for Reformation Research (1958–1963) in which position he organized a team to microfilm Reformation research materials in Germany and Zürich for use in the United States. Although he has had many articles published on the Reformation, his best-known work is *Luther and His Times*, from which this selection is taken.*

▶ # *The Background of the Times*

Martin Luther is one of those colossal historical figures over whom the modern world is still sharply divided, even though he died four centuries ago. Evaluations of his life and work range from those which see in him "the evil genius of Germany" to those which would make of him "a plaster saint."

It has been said that no one is really qualified to write on monasticism until he has been a monk; and after he has been a monk, he can no longer write impartially on monasticism. So, too, no one can really understand Martin Luther but a Lutheran; but perhaps no Lutheran can maintain a purely aca-

demic approach toward Luther. Yet it is encouraging that such scholars as Holl, Strohl, Scheel, and others have been able to approach Leopold von Ranke's ideal of writing history "as it actually was." This aim is well exemplified in James Harvey Robinson's prefatory remarks to Heinrich Boehmer's *Luther in the Light of Recent Research:* "The author seems to me particularly well qualified by knowledge, temperament and style to give us a fresh and stimulating conception of Luther. He is broadly sympathetic but no hero worshiper. There is no trace of religious partisanship in him. He feels that he can afford to tell all the varied

---

* Reprinted from E. G. Schwiebert, *Luther and His Times* (St. Louis, Mo.: Concordia Publishing House, 1950), pp. 1–11. Reprinted by permission of Concordia Publishing House, St. Louis, Missouri. Footnotes omitted.

truth without suppression or distortion."
To the historian there can be no higher
tribute.

Of all the periods in German history
none has been more diligently studied
than that of the German Reformation.
The many sermons, letters, political
treatises, and polemical tracts employ-
ing German, Latin, and some Greek
from Luther's pen appeared in nearly
a dozen editions between 1546 and 1883.
The related source materials, such as
court records, church documents, etc.,
which have appeared in print are tremendous. Over three thousand biographies and treatises have been written
about Martin Luther and his work, and
still they continue to roll from the
presses. Little wonder that few biogra-
phers of Luther have had the time or
patience to digest this mass of often
apparently contradictory materials before approaching their subject. The result is that all too frequently, both here
and abroad, there has been a tendency to
oversimplify the German Reformation.
A true evaluation of Luther's contributions to the world would require the
combined talents and training of a
linguist, political scientist, historian,
sociologist, and theologian, scarcely to
be found in a single individual.

Nor did Martin Luther bring about
the German Reformation single-
handedly. At his side labored twenty-
two university professors, many of whom
were equally zealous to reform the
Church. When Luther became convinced
that "justification by faith" was God's
plan of salvation, he did not rest until
he had won the whole faculty of the
University of Wittenberg to this point of
view. As will be seen in a later chapter,
this conversion was accomplished between 1513 and 1518.

When, therefore, Luther nailed his
Ninety-Five Theses on the door of the
Castle Church in Wittenberg, it was not
as an isolated individual, but with the
firm conviction that the entire university
faculty wanted the matter of indulgence
abuses clarified so as to establish a common principle of action in their midst.
This concerted action by the whole
group caused the University of Paris to
conclude a few years later that they were
dealing not with one "viper, but a whole
nest of vipers." The German Reformation was, then, an educational movement centered in the University of Wittenberg.

To be sure, the University was not yet
Lutheran in 1517, but remained nomi-
nally Roman Catholic until Luther was
pronounced a heretic by the Edict of
Worms in 1521. After that, all the conservative Catholic princes refused to support a school that kept on its faculty a
man condemned by both the Pope and
the Emperor. The enrollment dropped
tremendously in the next few years, owing to the withdrawal of the Catholic
support, leaving only the converts to the
reform movement. From this date, therefore, the *Album*, or matriculation book
of the University of Wittenberg, became
the mirror in which was reflected the
spread of Lutheranism in Central
Europe.

An examination of this interesting old
record in the library at Halle, Germany,
reveals that no fewer than 16,292 students enrolled at the University of Wittenberg between 1520 and 1560. Naturally, thousands of them left those
halls of learning with their souls on fire
for the new reform movement, which
they had heard so ably expounded at
the feet of Luther and Melanchthon.
The location of these students on the
map of Europe reveals that, even though
most of them came from German lands,

many of them came from England, France, Poland, the Scandinavian countries, and the Balkans. Who is to measure the impact of these thousands of Gospel preachers and teachers who returned to their home communities and became apostles of the Lutheran reform? The coming of the Reformation to each region, as reflected in the matriculation at the University of students from that territory, is a fascinating study.

Furthermore, it is significant how intimate was the contact between Luther and important men all over Europe. Any student familiar with his voluminous correspondence will need no further evidence. It is amazing that Luther, a busy professor, town pastor, civic leader, and author, was still able to keep his finger on the pulse of Germany. As for Melanchthon, it is claimed that he knew personally every schoolteacher in Germany who had been trained at Wittenberg.

In the light of these facts the German Reformation must be regarded as a very involved movement, the work not of Martin Luther and a few fellow professors, but of an army of people, some 22,000 students, priests, monks, and laymen carrying the Gospel message to the German people. Each community received the Reformation in its own unique way. In one region the message was brought by a Wittenberg layman; in another by a Catholic priest converted by Luther's writings; in a third by the sermon of some Wittenberg professor; but in every case we find that local conditions varied and the success of the movement in each community was determined by the ability of its leaders and the attitudes of those people to whom the message was brought. Thus the picture becomes almost kaleidoscopic in its confused complexity.

Nor does this new perspective detract from the glory of Luther; rather, it augments his place in the whole movement. In this setting Luther becomes the commander in chief of a vast army, while Melanchthon, Jonas, Amsdorf, Bugenhagen, and others make up his advisory staff. Fundamentally, then, the German Reformation was possible only because of a well-organized educational program that made Wittenberg the nursery of the whole movement.

The University assumed leadership in the church visitations, which so clearly exposed the deplorable conditions of ignorance and wickedness and the necessity for the organization of all types of schools throughout central Europe. In fact, it was the new Lutheranism produced in the parochial schools, the Latin schools, the boys' schools, the girls' schools, and the people's schools that caused the Reformation to triumph. And it was the counter-educational system of the Catholic Jesuits which rewon southern Germany.

If the work of Martin Luther could be reduced solely to the religious aspects of the German Reformation, the writing of his biography would be infinitely simpler. But Luther did not limit himself to the religious aspects of reform. His principle of "justification by faith" included a participation in civic affairs, which he ably expressed in the famous tracts of 1520. In his *Address to the German Nobility* of that year, Luther really became the voice of the Saxon court, appealing to the newly elected Emperor Charles V to reform the Church, since Rome had neglected its duty. In his *Babylonian Captivity of the Church* he expressed a maturity on the subject of indulgences that gave to men like Ulrich von Hutten a new hope that here was a champion of their common cause to liberate Germany from the economic and political bondage of the Roman See. In his statement of "the priesthood of believers," Luther destroyed the whole medieval concept of the divisions of society. In his tract of 1523, *Concerning Government: to What Extent One is Obligated to Obey It,* Luther defined the borderline between Church and State. One cannot, therefore, correctly evaluate Martin Luther's role in the sixteenth-century society without considering the impact of his advice and opinions on the attitudes and convictions of princes, prelates, and laymen.

To explain Luther's tremendous influence, one must consider also the value of the printing press and especially his use of that new medium, the *Flugschrift,* or tract. This new polemical vehicle had been employed in a lighter vein, but no one had thought of using it in the field of religion. Luther realized its possibilities as an inexpensive means of reaching the common man. Printed in the German language and attractively illustrated with woodcuts, it became an effective organ of reform by which he could reply in a few weeks to the attacks of his Roman opponents, or a medium for sermons, theological treatises, etc., all of which would familiarize the average layman with the Gospel movement. Its extensive use is shown by the fact that between 1517 and 1520 some 370 editions of his writings appeared, selling as many as 300,000 copies. Doubtless this was one of the major reasons why Luther succeeded where Hus had failed. The power of the printing press is shown in the report which Aleander, the papal representive at Worms in 1521, made in his dispatches to Leo X that nine tenths of Germany was shouting "Luther" and the other tenth "Down with Rome!"

This report, however, brings up an-other aspect of the German Reformation, on which must be sounded a word of warning. Aleander was wrong in assuming that all these enthusiastic supporters of Luther's cause were "Lutheran." It is true that the streets of Worms were crowded to the point where Luther could not pass directly from his quarters to the meetings of the Diet. According to contemporary reports, tremendous crowds greeted the Wittenberg monk on the way to and from Worms. But to assume that all these people held the theological views Luther was teaching at Wittenberg at the time is very wrong. Most of them were only vaguely conscious of the doctrines at stake, but felt that Luther was the champion of a people long bowed under the yoke of Rome. The common impression with laymen was that Martin Luther was the avowed opponent of the indulgence traffic of John Tetzel and the banking house of the Fuggers. Ulrich von Hutten thought he saw in Luther a powerful ally to liberate Germany from the yoke of Roman bondage, but failed completely to understand the deeper implications of Luther's controversy with the Roman Church. All the German princes, including even his bitter enemy Duke George, agreed with Luther in the belief that it was high time for the Diet to consider and act upon the *Gravamina,* the grievance lists drafted by previous diets from the days of Emperor Maximilian.

In addition, then, to the theological aspects of the Reformation, there were the economic, the political, and the social reforms which Luther's writings seemed to promise. As the reports of Aleander also indicate, many of the princes and even the counselors of the Emperor saw in Luther an opportunity to bring about economic and political changes long since overdue.

What Was the German Reformation?

Definitions are never too satisfactory; yet it may avoid considerable confusion to clarify certain accepted terminology. Textbook authors have employed several other terms than the older, more accepted usage, "The German Reformation." Some seem to prefer "The Protestant Revolt," others, "The Protestant Revolution." This is not just a matter of preference. Although perhaps not always aware of it, the writers using this terminology imply a definite basic assumption as to what the Reformation really was, and, therefore, these labels should be used with discrimination.

The term "Reformation" dates to a Cistercian monk, Joachim of Flora (d. 1202), who took the expression from the Latin Vulgate. He predicted that a new age was about to come in the Church, the Age of the Holy Ghost, and he made use of such terms as "New Life" and "Reformation," *nova vita* and *reformatio*, an idea which was continued by Dante and other Humanists. Humanism, then, through the revival of the classical languages, supplied the media for returning to earlier Christian standards. In such Biblical Humanists as Erasmus, Luther, and Melanchthon there developed a *Heimweh*, a longing for the pure forms of early Christianity.

Furthermore, the term "German Reformation" implies a special definition of the Church. In Roman circles the Church was defined as an outward ecclesiastical organization symbolized by the Papacy. In the new reasoning of Lutheranism there was implied something quite different. The Church was not an outward organization, but the *communio sanctorum*, the communion of saints, which had continued to live in the hearts of true believers, even though in outward forms Rome had drifted far from the original course. His many utterances on the subject reflect Luther's deep concern lest a corrupt outward organization create an environment unwholesome for God's elect. Hence, the word "Reformation" meant to Luther a cleansing of the outward Church of the Papacy, the Canon Law, the sacramental system, Scholasticism, saint worship, indulgences, and many other abuses and a restoration of the pure doctrines of the New Testament.

Nor did Martin Luther regard his undertaking as the establishment of a "New Church." Just six years before his death, Luther wrote a lengthy treatise, *On Councils and Churches*, proving by means of many illustrations from the Church Fathers and the early Ecumenical Councils that he had not founded a new Church, but rather that he had restored the "Early Church," the real Catholic Church, which preceded the Papacy. By comparison he ascertained that it was the Roman Church with its seven sacraments, its pope, and its hairsplitting theology that was new.

The use of the expression "Protestant Revolt," on the other hand, indicates a quite different basic assumption. It implies that the established Roman Catholic Church is the only true Church and that the founding of any other outward organization is a revolt against the divinely instituted authority. In fact, it implies that all those who revolted are now outside the pale of grace. If that is the intent of the historical writer, the use of this term is quite proper.

The expression "Protestant Revolution" has a similar implication, with more of a secular approach toward the whole movement. It implies little interest in, or understanding of, the deeper theological problems which were troubling the sixteenth-century mind. This reasoning places the center of gravity in economic, political, and sociological forces and assumes that they were more influential in shaping the course of events than theological differences.

Because Luther knew better than anyone else his views and objectives, and because he believed, as stated, that he sought only to cleanse and restore the early Christianity in all its purity, the term "Reformation" is most apropos; and because the birthplace of the movement was Germany, it may appropriately be designated the "German" Reformation.

The Need for Reform

In the days of Martin Luther it was a common error to consider the Papacy as synonymous with the Catholic Church. In fact, Catholic supporters of Rome, like Eck, Latomus, Emser, and Aleander, tried to identify the two in their polemical writings against Luther. Yet it does not follow that all Catholics of this period were of this opinion. As early as the fourteenth century such men as Wyclif, d'Ailly, Hus, Gerson, and a large body of northern Christians had taken issue with those who overemphasized the importance of the Roman hierarchy. The corruption of the Renaissance popes considerably augmented this number.

Previous to the Council of Trent (1545–1563) the Roman Church had no common system of dogma universally accepted by all the members of that body. In fact, the Roman Church might be compared to a huge edifice under whose roof a number of theological systems flourished. With the establishment of the universities there arose new scholars, capable of thinking independently of Rome, around whom developed distinct

and challenging schools of thought. In broad outlines, there were the Scholastics, the Mystics, and the Humanists, but more careful examination reveals that even these were often subdivided into separate schools. The followers of St. Thomas and those of William Occam had little in common; yet both were Scholastics. The Mystics all stressed emotion, but the different schools were not all in agreement with the views of Thomas à Kempis; while the Humanists, although all of them wanted to return to some "Golden Age," were far from agreed on what age this should be. Housed, therefore, under the roof of the Roman Church could be found widely divergent points of view. In some of the most fundamental doctrines these various schools expressed opposite points of view. One group believed in the doctrine of Transubstantiation, another in the Real Presence. In the University of Paris the importance of the Papacy had been minimized ever since the Reform Councils of the fifteenth century. For some time certain Catholic writers had stressed *Sola Scriptura*, the principle of making the Bible the sole guide in matters of faith. Bible reading had been emphasized by the Brethren of the Common Life. Such Biblical Humanists as Erasmus emphasized the need for a revival of Greek, Latin, and Hebrew so that scholars might examine the practices of the Roman Church in the light of early Christianity. There was, then, considerable disagreement among those who regarded themselves as Roman Catholics. In this fact lay one of the fundamental causes of the German Reformation.

It was this world of confusion into which Martin Luther was thrust when he entered the Augustinian monastery at Erfurt in 1505. The result was his tremendous soul struggle over the means of becoming reconciled with an angry and righteous God. After a wider study of the Catholic writings of the Middle Ages, Luther concluded that this was not the Christian Church established by the Apostles. In fact, with Erasmus and others Luther realized that early Christianity had been fundamentally quite different from the existing Roman Church.

The early Christian Church was a perfectly normal growth as the result of the teachings of Jesus and the Apostles. In the footsteps of missionaries like St. Paul and St. Peter, Christian communities sprang up all over the Roman Empire, which extended over an area nearly twice as large as the United States. Since there were no theological seminaries, most of the leaders in these communities were elders, men chosen from among the laymen for their fitness to read and to instruct others. Centers in which were capable leaders naturally lent aid to newer or less-favored communities and gradually assumed leadership of surrounding congregations. To their leader was given the name bishop, or *episcopus*. For some time these bishops were the leaders in this episcopal organization. In the second century, however, the larger communities covering the area of a Roman province were supervised by archbishops, and after the division of the Roman Empire by Emperor Diocletian in the third century the new heads of these vast areas were known as metropolitans. The idea of a papacy is, therefore, not a part of this early simple pattern of the Christian Church.

The simple, informal religion of the early Christians is also reflected in the basilica church, an unpretentious structure which they adapted from the Roman banks to ecclesiastical purposes. In this primitive church there was no railing between the worshipers and the altar, symbolic of the fact that the clergy was not yet regarded as a special order, the custodians of the means of grace. Nor can the historian find any traces of a papacy before the fourth century, and even then only in embryonic form.

From his studies Luther concluded that the real Christian Church was that *communio sanctorum*, or communion of true believers, which had existed from the first and which existed still in spite of the many human encrustations clinging to it. Others before him had arrived at this same conclusion. Some, like Erasmus, lacked the courage of their convictions. Others, like John Hus, died for their beliefs because the world was not ready. In Martin Luther the propitious moment and the qualities of leadership combined to produce the much-needed Reformation.

Those who have manifested an interest in the Anabaptist wing of the Reformation movement have usually come from its modern descendants such as present-day Baptists. GEORGE HUNSTON WILLIAMS (b. 1914) is one of these historians. He was trained at St. Lawrence University, Meadville Theological School, and Union Theological Seminary, New York. From 1947 to 1953 he was head of the history department of the Harvard Divinity School. He was named Winn Professor of Ecclesiastical History in 1956. Since 1963 he has been Hollis Professor of Divinity there. In *The Radical Reformation* (1962) he has sought to give the story of the more radical elements in the Reformation.*

Radical Elements in the Reformation

In the decade between the end of the sanguinary Great Peasants' War in Germany in 1525 and the collapse of the polygamous Biblical commonwealth of misguided peasants, artisans, and burghers in Münster in 1535, the gravest danger to an orderly and comprehensive reformation of Christendom was Anabaptism, which because of a profound disappointment with Martin Luther, Ulrich Zwingli, their clerical associates, and their magisterial supporters, withdrew into separatist conventicles. Anabaptists were regarded as seditious and heretical. The revival of the ancient Code of Justinian made this explicit. It was midway in the decade, at Speyer

in April 1529, in the same diet at which (April 19) six princes and the delegations of fourteen Upper German towns first took the name "Protestant" as stout adherents of Luther's reforms, that an imperial law (April 22) was published against the Anabaptists, in which both Catholics and "Protestants" concurred. The following day a mandate of Charles V gave specific instructions to the higher officials of the Empire as to how to deal with the baleful combination of sedition, schism, and heresy combated long ago in the ancient imperial laws against the Donatists and other separatists and willful puritans. For a brief season, however, the Anabaptists were in otherwise re-

---

* From *The Radical Reformation*, by George Hunston Williams. Copyright © 1962, W. L. Jenkins. The Westminster Press. Used by permission of the Westminster Press and Weidenfeld & Nicolson, Ltd. Pp. xxiii–xxxi.

spectable company, for the diet included in its censure also the sacramentarians, that is, the followers of Zwingli, because the Swiss seemed to be doing, in their interpretation and observance of the second of the two principal sacraments of the church—the Eucharist—what the Anabaptists were doing with the first—Baptism. By October of the same year, however, the Lutherans and the sacramentarians from Switzerland, along with representatives of the mediating position on the sacrament of the altar—notably, Martin Bucer of Strassburg—had met under the patronage of Landgrave Philip of Hesse at Marburg to compose the differences between the two reform movements issuing respectively from Wittenberg and Zurich. Although the two factions continued to disagree even violently on article 15 concerning the Lord's Supper, the over-all effect of the epoch-making colloquy was to extend the meaning of "Protestant" to include the Swiss and other pedobaptist sacramentarians. The Lutherans and the Zwinglians agreed at least, over against the Anabaptists, in interpreting the one sacrament, Baptism, as roughly equivalent to circumcision under the Old Covenant. They were alike disturbed by, and prepared to take stern measures against, the threat of the Anabaptists and the Spiritualists to the integrity and the durability of an orderly reformation with the sanction and support of the town councils, the princes, and the kings of Christendom. We may speak, therefore, of the Lutheran and Zwinglian movement and its analogues across the Channel and elsewhere as the Magisterial Reformation or, when one has in mind more its doctrine than its manner of establishment, as classical Protestantism.

It would be a mistake, of course, to assume that the theology of the Magis-terial Reformation was incapable of propagation without the assistance of magistrates: witness the extraordinary conquests of the Huguenots in Catholic France, the Helvetians in Catholic Poland, and the Calvinists in the rise of the Dutch Republic; nevertheless, Reformed Christians, wherever they were compelled to organize in a hostile environment, presupposed or proposed a truly Christian state, and always carried the seed of a complete Christian commonwealth within the temporary and protective husks of their clandestine conventicles. They did not, on principle, eschew fighting for the word of God, given a favorable conjuncture of events.

Over against magisterial Protestantism, and its *provisionally* "sectarian" outposts in Catholic lands, stood the Anabaptists, who, with their determination to clear away the old abuses root and branch and at the same time to dispense with earthly magistrates and prelates, were only the first major threat of what proved to be a three-pronged movement constituting the Radical Reformation, the further definition and delineation of which constitutes the burden of this book.

This Radical Reformation was a loosely interrelated congeries of reformations and restitutions which, besides the Anabaptists of various types, included Spiritualists and spiritualizers of varying tendencies, and the Evangelical Rationalists, largely Italian in origin. In contrast to the Protestants, the exponents of the Radical Reformation believed on principle in the separation of their own churches from the national or territorial state, although, in three or four instances (i.e., Müntzerites, Münsterites), they were misled into thinking that the regenerate magistrates from their own midst would prove more godly than Protestants or Catholics. With these exceptions, followers of the Radical Reformation in all three sectors denounced war and renounced all other forms of coercion except the ban, and sought to spread their version of the Christian life by missions, martyrdom, and philanthropy. No less confident than the fighting Calvinists that they were the chosen remnant of the Lord, having "through their covenant with God in a good conscience" worked out their own salvation in fear and trembling, these followers put their trust in the Lord of the quick and the dead, who would soon come and judge between the saints and the sinners.

In insisting on believers' baptism, or on the possession of the gifts of the Spirit, or on the experience of regeneration, and in being often quite indifferent to the general political and social order, the various exponents of the Radical Reformation not only opposed the Magisterial Reformation tactically and on principle but also clearly differentiated themselves from sixteenth-century Protestants, that is, the Lutherans and the Reformed (the Zwinglians and the Calvinists), on what constituted both the experience and the conception of salvation, and on what constituted the true church and proper Christian deportment. They saw in Luther's doctrine of salvation by faith alone a new indulgence system more grievous than that which he had attacked in ninety-five theses on the eve of the Reformation Era. They usually declined to use the theologically complementary term "sanctification," preferring, instead, to stress regeneration, or the new being in Christ, or the drive of the Spirit, or the quickening of the moral conscience, or, in veiled language, deification. In any event, the exponents and martyrs of the Radical Reformation, whether Anabaptists,

Spiritualists, or Rationalists, were alike in their dissatisfaction with the Lutheran-Zwinglian-Calvinist forensic formulation of justification and with any doctrine of original sin and predestination that seemed to them to undercut the significance of their personal religious experience and their continuous exercise of those personal and corporate disciplines by which they strove to imitate in their midst what they construed from the New Testament texts to have been the life of the original apostolic community.

From the *Enchiridion of the Christian Soldier* of Erasmus in 1504 and the Sacramentist *Epistola Christiana* of Cornelius Hoen, through Benedetto of Mantova's anthological *Benefit of Christ's Death*, to the *De Jesu Christo servatore* of Socinus in 1578, the whole tapestry of the Radical Reformation was interwoven with a loosely twined bundle of threads that were giving a new configuration to the doctrine of salvation. In this explicit or more often merely implicit reconstruction or replacement of the Anselmian doctrine of the atonement, there was a characteristic stress on the divine compassion and an elaboration of a devout and detailed doctrine of the *imitatio Christi* or the discipleship of the reborn Christian, a corresponding alteration in the doctrine of the incarnation (variously formulated in terms of the celestial flesh of Christ), and frequently also an alteration in the traditional formulations of the relationship of the Father and the Son. The variations in incarnational theology cut across the whole Radical Reformation. The various stages in the explicit opposition to the Nicene doctrine of the Trinity were largely limited to the Evangelical Rationalists. In their intense eschatological convictions, some of the Spiritualists, many

Anabaptists, and almost all of the Evangelical Rationalists adhered to the doctrine of the sleep or the death of the soul prior to the resurrection (psychopannychism).

The range and types of spirituality in the Radical Reformation suggest successively the rigor of the medieval monastery, the prim devotion of the Catholic Evangelicals, and the passion of the orders of the counter-reformed church far more than the hearty affirmation of life in all its vocational fullness that was characteristic of Lutheranism. Since there was, in fact, some continuity of Catholic Evangelism in Evangelical Rationalism, the brief interlude of Catholic Evangelism that burgeoned and then withered between 1500 and 1542 in the Romance lands has been included in the following account. Some of its early exponents joined the Protestants, others the Radical Reformation, while still others, after the introduction of the Roman Inquisition in 1542, turned their energies into the Counter Reform.

Constitutionally, the Radical Reformation was, of course, equally distant from classical (magisterial) Protestantism and Tridentine Catholicism. The reformers among the Old Believers and the Magisterial Reformers alike worked with the idea of *reformatio*; the Anabaptists, the Spiritualists, and the Rationalists labored under the more radical slogan of *restitutio*.

To be sure, the Protestants in their *reformatio* differed widely in the extent of their break from the medieval church.

To be specific, the progress of Lutheranism through a patchwork of territories and jurisdictions that seldom coincided even roughly with the medieval diocesan and provincial boundaries encouraged its leaders, in so many other respects conservative (where the Bible did not expressly speak against a traditional doctrinal formulation or institution), to minimize the significance of bishops and archbishops, so many of whom were, of course, temporal princes and thus integrally a part of the imperial constitution as prince-bishops and even imperial electors. With the expedient of the prince as *Notbischof*, Luther and his associates separated the whole question of polity from the core of essential Christian doctrine, although they were willing to utilize the office and traditions of episcopacy in organizing Lutheranism nationally, as in Sweden.

In contrast to Lutheranism, the Reformed churches (which began their career in breaking from episcopal authority with the sanction of the town councils) stressed polity as co-ordinate with doctrine; and, although basing the constitution of the Reformed Church (especially in Calvinism) on the polity of the New Testament, they unconsciously absorbed a good deal of the usage and political theory of the Swiss Conferedation of city republics and reworked ecclesiologically the civic institutions of local councils and diets.

Over against Lutheranism and the Reformed Church, Cranmerian Anglicanism preserved episcopacy on principle, but primarily as a constitutional necessity in the magisterial reformation of a national kingdom, with its lords temporal and lords spiritual in the upper house of its Parliament, interpreted as at once the national diet and the national synod. Only belatedly did Anglicanism turn to the task of providing the threefold ministry of deacons, priests, and bishops with an adequate theology of orders.

Though the Magisterial Reformation was far from unified in its conception of the sacraments in general and the place of polity in particular, it was one in the general conviction that behind the national, territorial, and the cantonal church organizations there existed the one holy Catholic Church, made up of the predestined saints (Calvin) or the assembly of the true believers (Luther).

In contrast to the three major expressions of the Magisterial Reformation, the proponents of the Radical Reformation, for the most part, rejected the doctrine of absolute predestination and the doctrine of an invisible church, and took seriously the ordering of their churches, conventicles, or fellowships of regenerate saints on the principle of voluntary association.

The proponents of the Radical Reformation, espousing the faithful restoration of the apostolic church as it existed in the age of the martyrs before it was prudentially supported by Constantine, differed among themselves, however, on the procedure for restoring or reassembling such a church. They also differed on the question of the constitutional significance for Christians of the role of the judges and the kings in the Scriptures of the Old Covenant.

Of the three radical groups, the Anabaptists were most confident in being able to reproduce the structure of apostolic Christianity from the New Testament, supplemented by texts they regarded as comparably primitive, or authoritative, for instance, the descriptions of the early churches preserved by Eusebius of Caesarea, a spurious epistle of Clement of Rome, and the works of early fathers. The Anabaptists differed among themselves as to the degree to which the pattern and institutions of the people of the Old Covenant and their Scriptures were appropriable. The Anabaptists of Münster, for example, with their eschatological intensity, easily combined the readings of Daniel in the Old Testament and Revelation in the New Testament and thereby justified their reintroduction of the Old Testament constitution of warrior saints.

The Spiritualists likewise differed among themselves in their use of the Bible as a pattern for the church. Thomas Müntzer, with his zeal for prophetic reform of the whole of society, like the Anabaptist Münsterites, used the Old Testament in his blueprints for the reformation of church and commonwealth.

The contemplative Spiritualist Casper Schwenckfeld, despairing of any valid *restitutio* without some clearer guidance from God than had been apparently given thus far, preferred, amidst the violent claims and counterclaims of Protestants, Catholics, and Anabaptists, to follow a "middle way" and to suspend the sacrament of the altar and interiorize it as an inward eucharist and communion until such a time as God himself would intervene and usher in the church of the Spirit. Other Spiritualists, such as the Libertines and isolated Rationalists, suspended the use of all the sacraments (forerunners in this respect of the Quakers).

The Evangelical Rationalists from Camillo Renato to Faustus Socinus tended to be individualistic in their Christianity and were, like the Evangelical Spiritualists, distressed by the divisiveness and acrimony attendant upon the organization of religion; and some might have preferred the half-enunciated ideal of Erasmus, namely, a "Third Church," neither Protestant nor Catholic, devout but not doctrinaire. In Poland, Lithuania, and Transylvania, the Evangelical Rationalist ferment permeated the local reformed churches to create three well-integrated and inwardly disciplined ecclesiastical bodies, one of them destined to survive intact to the present day as the Unitarian Church in Rumania.

The doctrine of the inwardly disciplined but externally free "apostolic" church has therefore been rightly recognized as one of the common marks of the whole of the Radical Reformation.

A consideration of ecclesiology and polity must, of course, include specific reference to the theory and practice of the ministry and ordination thereto. The fact that the proponents of the Radical Reformation were frequently laymen has obscured the no less interesting fact that the movement was in part re-ordinationist as well as in its main sector ana-baptist. Among the Magisterial Reformers there were several who, like Zwingli, having already been ordained under the *ancien régime*, declined on principle to be reordained on becoming Protestant.

In contrast, within the Radical Reformation there are several instances of former priests who felt the need for a recommissioning and who finally repudiated their Catholic ordination (e.g., Menno Simons). In other instances, leaders to the end were obsessed with the question of a valid apostolic vocation, that is, the problem of being authentically sent to proclaim, to baptize, and to organize in the latter days of the world (e.g., Obbe Philips). In some cases the Radical Reformation leaders seemed to connect the continuity of missionary authority with the baptismal succession, at times with the direct outpouring of the Spirit. Thus, though many "lay" leaders within the Radical Reformation, such as Conrad Grebel, Schwenckfeld, and Socinus, were, so far as we know, never formally ordained, to overstress this would obscure the fact that the credentials of leadership in the Radical Reformation were at the beginning more often moral or charismatic than regular. The strongly re-ordinationist thrust within the Radical Reformation would, needless to say, become explicit only in the relatively few instances when a cleric of the old order became a leader in the new. Unordained monks and friars were, however, much more common among the recruits of the Radical Reformation than were ordained priests and prelates. Thus, a basic conflict over the conception of the nature of the church and polity between the Radical Reformation and the Magisterial Reformation came to be articulated in the debate between the two sides, not in terms of ordination, which was generally neglected, but rather in terms of formal, university theological education on the one side and apostolic, or prophetic or inspired, vocation on the other.

Akin to the prominence of the layman in the Radical Reformation and the functional extension of the priesthood of all believers in the direction of personal witness to Christ in missions and martyrdom, rather than in the diversification of the conception of vocation (as with Luther and Calvin), was the corresponding elevation of women to a status of almost complete equality with men in the central task of the fellowship of the reborn. Correlative with the enhanced role of women was the reconception of the medieval sacrament of marriage in the covenantal context of the Radical Reformation.

So much, then, by way of introduction for some of the traits common to the Radical Reformation.

Modern, and particularly American, Protestants, seeking to grasp the Radical Reformation as a whole, must try to see it as one of the two fronts against which classical Protestantism was seeking to establish its position, the other being Catholicism, which was renewing its strength and extending its global bounds.

With what they considered the papal Antichrist to their right, Luther and Melanchthon, Zwingli then Bullinger, Calvin and Cranmer, readily thought of their common foe to the left as a three-headed Cerberus and called the monster abusingly, without their wonted theological precision, almost interchangeably Libertinism, Anabaptism, Fanaticism. Today we are in a position to see much more clearly than they did the differences within the Radical Reformation. Indeed, historians within the denominational traditions surviving intact from the age of their martyrs, namely, the Mennonites, the Hutterites, the Schwenckfelders, and the (Transylvanian) Unitarians, and others in traditions indirectly dependent upon it—namely, the Quakers and the Baptists—have gone so far in the direction of distinguishing in the sixteenth century the Anabaptists and the Spiritualists and the Evangelical Rationalists that there is once again a great need to see the whole of the Radical Reformation synoptically, the better to understand both the general morphology of Christian radicalism and the classical formulation of Protestantism.

As a variegated episode in the general history of Christianity, the Radical Reformation may be said to extend from 1516, the year of Erasmus' edition of the Greek New Testament, to a cluster of events around 1578 and 1579, namely, the death of the leader of the Hutterites in their golden age (Peter Walpot); the death of the leader of the Transylvanian Unitarians (Francis Dávid); the arrival of Faustus Socinus in Poland and his conversion of Racovian, anti-Trinitarian Anabaptism in the direction of Socinianism; the official toleration of Mennonitism by William of Orange; and the Emden disputation between the Mennonites and the Reformed. By rougly this time, the Radical Reformation had eliminated its most obvious excesses, had softened its asperities, and had, moreover, come to differentiate and redefine quite clearly its own disparate impulses, settling down and consolidating inwardly in diverse and largely isolated sects and fellowships. Slowly gathering strength, bearers of their ideas and institutions or groups analogous to them were to become once again involved in general history, notably in the restructuring of English Christendom in the age of the Civil Wars and the Commonwealth. Again in our own times, when, in a new context at once secular and ecumenical, the European state churches are being disestablished, the large churchlike American denominations are being reorganized, and the younger churches of Asia and Africa are being challenged by renascent ethnic religions and the international religion of the proletariat, when, in short, the mission of the churches everywhere is being reconceived in a basically hostile or alienated environment, Christians of many denominations are finding themselves constitutionally and in certain other ways closer to the descendants of the despised sectaries of the Reformation Era than to the classical defenders of a reformed *corpus christianum*.

ROLAND H. BAINTON (b. 1894), of Baptist origins, has devoted much of his life to the study of the more radical elements in the Reformation, showing particular interest in some of those who specifically opposed Protestant leaders such as Calvin. Trained in the United States, he became the Titus Street Professor of Ecclesiastical History at Yale University in 1936, and in that position has wielded an important influence on the study of the church history, particularly on the interpretation of the Reformation. The analysis of the movement as a whole which he presents here has a special interest as it represents much of the current Protestant thinking on the subject.*

The Complexity of the Reformation

The Sixteenth Century The sixteenth century was the Age of the Reformation. It was, of course, the age of much else besides. It might also be called the Age of Discovery, for in the wake of the *Santa Maria* there came the navigators and the conquistadores. Nevertheless, in the sixteenth century the New World had not as yet made a decisive impact upon the Old. The effect may have been greatest in the economic sphere through the influx of bullion from the Spanish possessions, but not until the seventeenth century did the Americas, to any large degree, offer an asylum to the oppressed, an area for social and political experimentation to the hardy, and an opportunity for improvement to the disinherited of Europe.

The sixteenth century was also an age of sciences and more so than the preceding one hundred years. In fact, if one can talk of the Renaissance in science, it must be placed a century after the great flowering of art and letters in Italy of the fifteenth and early sixteenth centuries. Curiously, the year which in Church history may be taken to demarcate the Renaissance from the Counterreformation, the year 1542 which saw the establishment of the Roman Inquisition was the very year of the publication of the *Anatomy* of Vesalius and the year following, 1543, saw the appearance of

---

* Reprinted from Roland H. Bainton, *The Age of the Reformation* (Princeton, N.J.: D. Van Nostrand Company, Inc., 1956), pp. 11–22. Footnotes omitted.

the work of Copernicus, *On the Revolution of the Heavenly Spheres*. Yet, despite these and other great discoveries, the sixteenth century cannot properly be called the age of science. The full impact of the new findings was not to be felt until later, for in the 1500's men did not look to natural science to solve the problems and answer the riddles of life, nor was there as yet a great crisis in Christendom over the conflict of science and religion. As late as the eighteenth century, theologians as well as scientists believed that the astronomers in particular were but thinking God's thoughts after Him. Only in the nineteenth century did geology and biology relegate Genesis to religious mythology.

The sixteenth century was an age of faith. It was even more an age of faith than the preceding period. For a parallel, one must go back several hundred years to the days of the First Crusade or even to the founding of the Inquisition. In the period of the Reformation men were ready both to die and to kill for religion, to divide families and to disrupt kingdoms rather than renounce the truth of God. The Reformation actually arrested an incipient secularism and made religion and even confessionalism dominant concerns even in politics for another 150 years.

The Reformation was both Protestant and Catholic. The two parties to this day are not at one in their interpretation of the events. The Protestants call the Catholic Reformation the Counterreformation. To a degree it was, because manifestly it opposed the Protestant Reformation and incontestably was stimulated by it, but did not originate out of opposition, for a Catholic reformation was underway before the emergence of Luther and at the peak was not wholly consumed in counter measures. One of the great endeavors of the Catholic Reformation was the evangelization of the New World. The Catholics, in turn, sometimes call their movement The Reformation and the Protestant the Pseudoreformation. Obviously, the historian of this period is not poking ashes without embers, and he does well at the outset to avow his own affiliation. The writer of this book is a staunch Protestant. At the same time he kneels before the shrine of historical objectivity. Let it be hoped that the two are not mutually exclusive.

Causes of the Reformation　There are three schools of interpretation with regard to the origins of the Reformation, particularly in its Protestant form. The first is moral, the second doctrinal, and the third sociological. The first maintains the basic cause of the Reformation in all its forms to have been the undeniable moral corruption of the Church. Some Catholic historians have contended that the Protestant Reformation was a continuation of the abuses through the abrogation of the rules. Clerical concubinage, for example, was ended not by clerical celibacy but by clerical marriage. Other Catholic historians have said that the early Protestants were passionate moral reformers whose inordinate zeal carried them beyond the bounds of obedience.

Another school maintains that the correction of moral corruption was only an incidental concern of Luther and his associates. The attack was rather against the teaching of the Church. In general this has been a Protestant interpretation, though recently some Catholic historians concur. The Catholic Reformation, of course, also involved doctrine. The third school looks more to changes in the structure of society, urbanization, commercialism and nationalism, adjustment to which on the part of the Church occasioned convulsions of diverse sorts.

As to the first approach: moral abuses unquestionably concerned all of the reformers, whether Catholic or Protestant. The difference was as to precisely what should be considered an abuse and what should be the remedy. At this point a memorandum compiled by the Cardinals and submitted to Pope Paul III in 1538 on *The Reform of the Church* may be instructively compared with Luther's arraignment in his *Address to the Christian Nobility of the German Nation.*

The Cardinals centered on abuses parochial, financial, judicial, and moral. As to the parochial: the cure of souls, complained the Cardinals, was neglected because unworthy and uninstructed candidates were ordained to the ministry. Foreigners were given sees they could not serve, and many of the clergy were constantly nonresident. On the financial side objection was registered against pluralities, i.e., the conferring on one person of several income-yielding benefices; also against expectations whereby for a fee an expectancy was granted to a see not yet vacant, and likewise against commutations whereby a vow was remitted in favor of a financial contribution. General reference was made to simony which is strictly the buying of any ecclesiastical office. The dispensing of indulgences should be, said the Cardinals, restricted to once a year in a single locality. In the judicial sphere complaint was made of dispensations whereby again for a fee exemption was granted from the laws of the Church. The great moral abuse was the position of honor accorded prostitutes in Rome. Doctrinal abuses were held not to exist because the teaching of the Church is inerrant. The only concern was that the truth should not be corrupted by the teaching of sceptical professors, nor suborned by the unedifying *Colloquies* of Erasmus.

Luther was more caustic and devastating partly because he was voicing the century-old complaints of the Germans against the exploitation of their land by Italian Popes. His indictment of the pomp, luxury, and extravagance of the heads of the Church, including the Cardinals, was naturally more trenchant than the complaints emanating from the Sacred College, though there was much agreement, notably with regard to the neglect of the cure of souls and as to the judicial abuses. Luther went further in his demand for the restriction of appeals; on the matter of sexual immorality the Cardinals referred only to the prostitutes at Rome and made no mention of the system of clerical concubinage, tolerated and taxed, which Luther excoriated. The difference is most significant at the point of the remedy. The Cardinals would enforce the rule of celibacy for the clergy. Luther would abolish the rule and allow clerical marriage.

Yet, for Luther this was not the primary ground of objection. He said himself that what differentiated him from previous reformers was that, whereas they attacked the life, he attacked the doctrine. By so doing he compelled the Catholics to reexamine and more tightly formulate their own position. The Catholic answer was to displace the prevalent scholastic theology by another of an earlier vintage. Occamism, then popularly called Modernism, was displaced by Thomism. A word with regard to these two systems. The Thomistic position is that all truth can be rationally integrated by a system of ascending levels. The natural man by his reason and conscience can attain to the knowledge of the God and can apprehend that universal morality called natural law. The higher reaches of theology, including God's trinitarian structure, are attainable only by revelation, just as the loftier Christian virtues require the assistance of special divine grace, but nature leads up to grace and reason to revelation which, once given, can be explicated by reason. The entire structure of theology, the Church, and society is further integrated by the assumption that reality consists of universals, i.e., entities which embrace and relate particular manifestations. The Church and the State and even the Trinity are not aggregates of unrelated individuals but are gathered rather in a nexus of corporate being.

This theology was challenged by Occamism. It denied the universals, claiming rather that reality consists of particular single individuals related only by contiguity in space and time. Consequently the State is not a universal corporate entity but only the sum of its citizens; likewise the Church of its members. On this assumption the State tends to be based on contract between members, and the Church on covenant. When this view is applied to the Trinity, if the three persons are individuals related only by contiguity in space and time, then they become three gods. Such was the answer of philosophy, but since the Church had ruled that they are not three gods, theology and philosophy must diverge. The result is the doctrine of double truth or at least of double logic. The teaching of the Church no longer supported by reason was compelled therefore to fall back on arbitrary authority. This Modernism the Catholic Reformation rejected and reverted to Thomism.

Some Catholic interpreters agree that the Protestant Reformation was doctrinal in the sense that it was derived from scholastic Modernism. Basically this is not so. The individualism of Luther was of another sort, as we shall see. He had been trained as a Modernist, to be sure, but he was not interested, at bottom, in philosophy at all. Greater weight may be given to the claim that he was influenced by this movement to locate authority in the Bible. Even here, however, what else could he have done, when he rejected the authority of the Church, other than to appeal to the authority of the Scriptures?

Yet Luther's Reformation was doctrinal because it was profoundly religious. Not so much the ideas of Modernism repelled him as the temperature. His development will be more fully delineated in the next section, but the difference can well be illustrated now by taking the case of indulgences. They were introduced at the time of the Crusades. First, those who took the cross were accorded whatever merits would have accrued had they stayed at home and engaged in some pious exercise such as a pilgrimage. Next, indulgences were granted to those who, unable to go on a Crusade, made a money contribution. Such persons in return might receive a remission of penalties imposed upon them by the Church. The device proved so lucrative that it was extended to every worthy object such as the building of cathedrals, hospitals, and even bridges. The noblest monuments of the Middle Ages were financed in this way. In the meantime, claims for indulgences were staggered. They were made to apply not only to penalties on earth but also in purgatory. Persons already in purgatory might be granted immediate release. Some indulgences remitted not only penalties but also forgave sins. The theory on which the entire practice rested was that the Pope held the key to the treasury of the merits of the saints, who having been better than they needed to be for their own salvation, had acquired a store of superfluous credits and these were regarded as transferable to others. Plainly the practice ministered to venality. This the Cardinals, addressing Pope Paul III, would curb by allowing but one vending of indulgences a year in the same locality, but Luther's objection was vastly more drastic. He denied the treasury of the accumulated, superfluous merits of the saints. After all of the financial abuses were corrected, he still regarded the entire transaction as an abomination. What he demanded was not reform but abolition. Not merely the practice but also the teaching was at fault, and not simply was it false but an abomination in the eyes of God.

The Sociological Background The third school of modern historians would interpret the Reformation less in moral and doctrinal than in sociological terms. A recent author has outlined the changes in the structure of society and the accommodations of the Catholic Church during the period of the Renaissance. There was taking place, he suggests, "a transition from a civilization predominantly feudal and ecclesiastical in its social, political and cultural manifestations and agrarian in its foundations, to another predominantly national, urban, secular and laic, in which the economic center of gravity had shifted from agriculture to commerce and industry and in which a simple money economy had evolved into capitalism."

The attempt of the Church to adjust to the new urban economy based on coin rather than on kind gave rise to some of the financial abuses already enumerated, and conflicts with the national states over money entailed political changes. The immediate produce of the land had been the basis of the Church's financial structure in the early Middle Ages. The Church could scarcely have operated otherwise in a landed society, but the consequence was entanglement in the feudal system with the danger of dependence on lay lords. The new economy offered a way to obviate this by drawing revenues not directly from lands often in lay hands but through levies on the local churches to be paid in coin. To this, however, the rising national monarchies objected, and in the first instance France. The papacy, depleted of resources, succumbed to France, and the residence of the Popes was transferred to Avignon for a period called the Babylonian Captivity because it was roughly seventy years in duration (1309–1377).

During that period the attempt continued unabated to centralize the wealth of the Church by levies on the local sees. Pope John XXII, in particular, exploited and devised such expedients as annates, reservations, expectations, commutations and others, and the French crown objected little, inasmuch as the money was not to cross the Alps. The subjection of the papacy to France, however, occasioned such disaffection in other lands that the secession manifest in the Protestant Reformation was in danger of anticipation by some 200 years. To avert this the Pope returned to Rome. The Cardinals, however, remained in France and elected another Pope. There followed the Papal Schism lasting until 1417. Attempts were made to end the scandal by the summoning of councils, and they in turn undertook the reform of the Church, but every effort proved abortive. Conciliarism was impotent because the conflict with the rising, consolidated, national monarchies required an increasingly centralized government on the side of the Church. In the end the papacy overcame conciliarism, but only at the price of recognizing the sovereignty of the national states. Conceding this, the Popes then made separate bargains called concordats with the nations.

All of this involved a great recession from the universal claim and the universal jurisdiction which the Church had once exercised at the peak of the feudal period. By way of compensation the Church in the Renaissance entrenched itself in Italy. The papacy became one of the Italian powers, and the Popes behaved like the despots of the city-states, cunning in diplomacy, ruthless in war, magnificent in the arts and literature, unscrupulous and unbridled in morals. The reform movements were set over against a thoroughgoing secularization of the papacy itself. The Pope who dealt with Martin Luther, Leo X, was an elegant dilettante, a patron of artists, a gambler, hunter, and composer of elegant, impromptu Latin orations, a man who, according to a modern Catholic historian, would not have been deemed fit to be a doorkeeper in the house of the Lord had he lived in the days of the apostles.

In the social changes outlined above, some would see the basic ground of the Reformation, involving on the Catholic side a grudging relinquishment of medieval claims, a recognition of nationalism, and even a nationalizing of the Church, which in France and Spain fell under the control of the crown.

Protestantism took on the complexion of the land in which it chanced to be. With complete opportunism alliances were made with whatever power offered protection to the Word of God. This might mean Tudor absolutism, German particularism, Polish feudalism, or even extra-Europeanism under the suzerainty of the infidel Turks. The Protestants were politically conservative and only slowly and reluctantly resisted the political regimes of the particular countries. As for the control of the Church over the civil structure of society Luther renounced all this, but Calvin struck out in the direction of a new type of theocracy.

The foregoing picture of the changes taking place in the society cannot be gainsaid and, unquestionably, the Church did have to come to terms with urbanization, commercialization, nationalism, and the emergence of a lay and secular culture, but the Reformation, whether Catholic or Protestant, is not to be equated with the accommodation which, in many instances, was grudging and, when cordial, was transforming. Consider the case of lay culture, which the Catholic Reformation naturally did not foster. Instead it enhanced sacerdotalism. Protestantism did contribute to laicism but not to secularism. The priesthood of all believers was designed not to make all priests into laymen, but all laymen into priests. The net result, of course, was to demote the clerical caste, but not to diminish the religious orientation. The Protestants desired that every member of the congregation should be as spiritual and, in so far as might be possible, as instructed in matters religious as the ministers. The Jesuits undertook the education of the Catholic masses that the laity might be religiously literate.

More attention will be given in this book to the Protestant than to the Catholic Reformation. The reason is that the Protestant movement did more to change the face of Europe. The Catholic Reformation was endeavoring to correct defections from its own ideal and to restore a waning control. The Protestants sought to alter the pattern. The hope was that all Christendom would embrace the new. The result was a shattered ecclesiastical structure. The relations of Church and State were profoundly affected. In the process of adjustment arose wars of religion—wars, at any rate, in which religion was a major component. Out of all the welter emerged new attitudes to life and to religion.

Anticipations of the Reformation
The Protestant Reformation was not without its antecedents, not even at the point of the disruption of Christendom. One must not forget that the Roman Church had long since been separate from the Greek and the Russian, not to mention the smaller Eastern dissidents. The Reformation affected only the West, and even in the West the Protestant secession was but the culmination of a long series of schisms during the preceding 300 years. Curiously, the peak of the Church's theocratic control was also the period of incipient disintegration. In the age of Innocent III, when the Pope exercised a control, albeit indirect, exceeding that of any king even in matters political, at that very moment Christendom was challenged at the center by the infiltration of the Catharan heresy into southern France. In the same region and in northern Italy flourished the Waldenses. The sectarian swarm anticipated the pattern of later Protestantism at its most divisive moments. Northern Italy was in particular infested by the Patarini, Petrobrusiani, Arnoldisti, Tisserands, Humiliati and Fraticelli. In England the Lollards presaged an ecclesiastical revolution and in Bohemia the Hussites achieved one. Of all these groups only the Waldenses survived by

retreat into the recesses of the Alps and the Hussites by force of arms in Bohemia. The Protestant Reformation does not stem directly from any of these sects. Yet the virulent critique which the sectaries had long hurled at the established Church cannot wholly be discounted as preparing the public mind.

Many of the ideas of the medieval sects fed at least indirectly into Protestantism in its various phases. One was moralism. Some of the earlier reformers contended that the very sacraments of the Church are invalid if administered by the unworthy. The Catholic Church holds, on the contrary, that the efficacy is of God and the unworthiness of the human ministrant in no way detracts. Yet the reformatory Pope, Gregory VII, had played into the hands of the insurgents by calling upon the laity to refuse to receive the sacraments at the hands of the married clergy. He did not say that the sacraments would do no good, only that they should be rejected in order to rebuke the ministrant. The inference, however, was not far off that misdeeds would invalidate the act.

Another subversive idea was predestination, the doctrine that some have been elected by God from before the very foundation of the world and that they are the true Church. This idea is not disruptive if there is absolutely no way of telling who are the elect, but if a worthy life be an indication of election and if an unworthy life be a fairly certain sign of reprobation, if, in other words, predestination be combined with moralism, then the deduction is obvious that a scandalous Pope does not even belong to the true Church at all. Such was the conclusion of John Wyclif.

Predestination undercut the Church from one direction. Eschatology, the doctrine of last things, assailed the Church from another. The latter was the belief in the speedy return of the Lord Jesus. Catholicism, from the days of St. Augustine, had projected the second coming of Christ indefinitely into the future and had centered attention upon the confrontation of the individual soul with its judge at the Last Day. The new eschatology weakened the authority of the great medieval theocracy by the announcement that its term was short and, if unreformed, its doom was sure. Such ideas are found among the Spiritual Franciscans and the Hussites.

Many of the sectaries attacked the theory of the sacraments, particularly of the Mass. The Fourth Lateran Council in the age of Innocent III had formulated the doctrine of transubstantiation, according to which, when the priest pronounces the words *Hoc est corpus meum*, "this is my body," the bread and the wine on the altar continue to look, taste, and feel as before. Their accidents remain the same, but their substance changes into the substance of the flesh and blood of Christ. The priest offers again this flesh and blood as a sacrifice to God, and Calvary is thus repeated. Only the priest can perform this miracle because only he is qualified through the sacrament of ordination. Inasmuch as salvation is mediated through the sacraments the priest therefore occupies a unique position. Since he is able to do for men more even than their earthly parents, who generate them only to temporal life, whereas he begets them to the eternal, his power exceeds that of any monarch who rules only over the body and not over the soul. And by virtue of this spiritual prerogative the priest acquires a right to direct, in many respects, the lives of men. To deny, then, that the Sacrament of the Mass actually brings Christ physically to the altar, to

deny that the sacrifice of Calvary is repeated, to deny that the priest alone can do whatever is done, any and all of these denials demote the Church in things spiritual and temporal. Transubstantiation was denied by the Cathari, the Wyclifites and the Waldenses, and the lay element was stressed by all.

The authority of the Church was challenged from more than one angle. The Franciscans, dedicated to absolute poverty, lodged a charge of heresy against that money-raising Pope, John XXII, because of his declaration that Christ had property. The Modernists in philosophy sorely needed authority to undergird theology, but where was authority to be discovered? It could not reside in the great entities called universals of which the Church itself was one but only in individuals. But could the Pope as an individual be regarded as infallible? A negative answer was given by William of Occam who was at once the founder of the Modernists and also a Franciscan. He lived in the days of Pope John XXII and compiled a massive compendium of his errors. Occam concluded that since the gates of hell cannot prevail against the Church, someone always in the Church will be right, but there is no infallible way of knowing who it may be. The only recourse is to rely upon the authority of the Bible.

The Bible, however, was subjected to historical criticism by the Humanists, the scholars of the Renaissance. They began investigating the manuscripts and revising the texts. The greatest among them was Erasmus of Rotterdam who in his edition of the Greek New Testament in 1516—the very first printing of the New Testament in Greek—left out the famous text in First John 5: "There are three that witness in Heaven, the Father, the Spirit, and the Son," which he was unable to find in any manuscript. He promised when challenged to insert it in subsequent editions if a single manuscript could be found in which it occurred. His condition was met from a very late copy and he fulfilled his word in the third edition of 1521. Still he was unconvinced and the Church had eventually to recognize he had been right at the outset. But this meant that not the Pope but an historical expert must determine the text of the Scripture and how then could the Pope be an infallible interpreter if he were not in a position to determine the true text? In this period, of course, the Pope had not been infallibly declared to be infallible. The assumption was, however, already common.

Again there were those among the Humanists and the Mystics such as the Brethren of the Common Life and the Friends of God who centered piety on the love of God and the service of the neighbor in the imitation of the lowly Jesus. They decried theological speculation. Such a position was not in conflict with the teachings of the Church, only indifferent to certain aspects. Yet such a view meant that Thomism would have to be regarded as inconsequential and the emphasis upon the imitation of Christ was a standing rebuke to churchmen who behaved more like the rulers of the Gentiles. The sectaries such as Wyclif and Hus were particularly fond of drawing a disparaging contrast between Christ refusing a crown and the Pope wearing a three-tiered tiara, more imposing than the single-layered crown of an emperor.

MARTIN J. SPALDING (1810–1872) was a
prominent member of the American Roman Catholic
Hierarchy during the nineteenth century and a
scholar of some importance. A graduate of St. Mary's
College, he received his Doctor of Divinity degree
from Urban College, Rome, in 1830 and in 1835
became editor of the *Catholic Advocate*. After holding
the position of rector of St. Joseph's College for two
years, he was made Bishop of Louisville in 1848 and
in 1864 became Archbishop of Baltimore, a position
he occupied until his death. A leading American
Roman Catholic theologian, he did much to forward
Roman Catholic education in the United States and
helped to found the American College at Louvain,
Belgium. During Vatican Council I (1870–1871)
he played an important part in the debates.*

▶ # *Merle d'Aubigné's Views Challenged*

We are now to examine what was the
character of the work itself [the Refor-
mation], and how it was accomplished.
Were the reasons which were assigned,
as the principal motives for this alleged
reform in religion, sufficient to justify
it, according to the judgment of im-
partial men? Were the means employed
for bringing it about such as would lead
us to believe, that it was really a change
for the better; and were they such as
God would or could have approved and
sanctioned? Finally, weighing these motives and these means, and making all
due allowance for the condition of the
times, was there any thing very remarkable in the rapid progress of the Ref-

ormation itself? We will endeavor to
answer these questions . . .

D'Aubigné, and those who concur
with him, profess to believe, or at least
endeavor to make others believe, that
the Reformation was not only sanctioned
by God, but that it was directly His
work. He says:

"Christianity and the Reformation are,
indeed, the same revolution, but working at
different periods, and in dissimilar circumstances. They differ in secondary features—
they are alike in their first lines, and leading
characteristics. The one is the reappearance
of the other. The former closes the old order
of things—the latter begins the new. Between them is the middle age. One is the

---

* Reprinted from Martin J. Spalding, *The History of the Protestant Reformation* (Louisville, Ky., 1860), vol. I, pp. 102–109. Footnotes omitted.

parent of the other; and if the daughter is in some respects inferior, she has, in others, characters altogether peculiar to herself."

In opposition to this flattering theory, we will endeavor to prove that the Reformation differs from Christianity, not only "in secondary features," but also "in its first lines and leading characteristics;" and that, if the former was the daughter of the latter, she was a most recreant and degenerate daughter truly, with scarcely one lineament in common with her parent. Verily, she had "characters altogether peculiar to herself," and she was not only "in some respects," but in almost every thing, not only "inferior" to, but the direct opposite, of her alleged parent!

According to our author, one of these "characters of the Reformation peculiar to itself," was "the suddenness of its action." He illustrates the rapidity with which the Reformation was established, by the figure employed by our blessed Saviour to denote the suddenness of His second coming: "As the lightning cometh forth from the west and shineth to the east, so shall also the coming of the Son of man be." "Christianity," he says, "was one of those revolutions, which was slowly and gradually prepared;" the Reformation, on the contrary, was instantaneous in its effect:— "A monk speaks, and in half of Europe the power and glory [of the Church of Rome] crumbles in the dust!" This rapidity he views as a certain evidence, that the Reformation was assuredly the work of God. For "how could an entire people—how could so many nations, have so rapidly performed so difficult a work? How could such an act of critical judgment [on the necessity and measure of the reform] kindle the enthusiasm indispensable to great, and especially to

sudden revolutions? But the Reformation was a work of a very different kind; and this, its history will prove. It was the pouring forth anew of that life which Christianity had brought into the world."

We trust to make it appear in the sequel, that the rapidity with which the Reformation was diffused, was the result of the pouring forth of a different spirit altogether. Meantime we would beg leave to ask D'Aubigné to answer this plain argument, specially adapted to the case as he puts it: if the suddenness of the Reformation be a proof that it was brought about by the "pouring forth anew of that life which Christianity had brought into the world;" would not the contrary feature of Christianity—its gradual operation—be a conclusive evidence, that this latter system was not the work of God? And if this argument be not valid, what truth is there in D'Aubigné's entire theory? Would not his reasoning, if reduced to the strict laws of logic, rather prove, on the contrary, if it proved any thing, that the Reformation, differing avowedly as it does in an essential feature from Christianity, was not effected by the Holy Spirit, but was the mere result of violent human passions, which usually bring about sudden revolutions, both in the religious and in the social system?

It is curious to trace the further development of his favorite theory.

"Two considerations will account for the rapidity and extent of this revolution. One of these must be sought in God, the other among men. The impulse was given by an unseen hand of power, and the change which took place was the work of God. This will be the conclusion arrived at by every one who considers the subject with impartiality and attention, and does not rest in a superficial view. But the historian has a further office to perform—God acts by second causes. Many circumstances, which have often escaped observation, gradually prepared men for the great transformation of the sixteenth century, so that the human mind was ripe when the hour of its emancipation arrived."

Now, we have given no little attention to the subject, and we claim at least as much impartiality as our historian of "the great Reformation;" and yet, with the facts of history before us, we can arrive at no such conclusion, but have reached one precisely contrary. And the reasons which have forced us to draw this latter inference are so many and so cogent, that we are even under the conviction, that no one who will "consider the subject with impartiality and attention, and does not rest in a superficial view," can fail to agree with us.

In examining the secondary causes, by which God "gradually prepared men for the great transformation of the sixteenth century," our historian assigns a prominent place to the central and commanding position of Germany.

"As Judea, the birth-place of our religion, lay in the centre of the ancient world, so Germany was situate in the midst of Christian nations. She looked upon the Netherlands, England, France, Switzerland, Italy, Hungary, Bohemia, Poland, Denmark, and the whole of the north. It was fit that the principle of life should develop itself in the *heart* of Europe, that its pulses might circulate through all the arteries of the body the generous blood designed to vivify its members."

He alleges the following most singular reasons why Germany was prepared for embracing the Reformation:

"The Germans had received from Rome that element of modern civilization, the faith. Instruction, legislation—all, save their

courage and their weapons, had come to them from the sacerdotal city. Strong ties had from that time attached Germany to the Papacy."—Therefore was she "ripe" for a rupture with Rome! This connexion with Rome "made the reaction more powerful at the moment of awakening."

Again: "The gospel had never been offered to Germany in its primitive purity; the first missionaries who visited the country gave to it a religion already vitiated in more than one particular. It was a law of the Church, a spiritual discipline, that Boniface and his successors carried to the Frisons, the Saxons, and other German nations. Faith in the 'good tidings,' that faith which rejoices the heart and makes it free indeed, had remained unknown to them."—Therefore, when Luther and his brother reformers announced these "good tidings" in all their purity for the first time—fraught too with endless variations and contradictions—The Germans were prepared for the "awakening," and received the gospel with enthusiasm!! Truly, our fanciful and romantic historian loves to reason by contraries, and to startle his readers by palpable absurdities!

No less curious is his reason for explaining why the Italians did not receive the new gospel:

"And if the truth was destined to come from the north, how could the Italians, so enlightened, of so refined a taste and social habits, so delicate in their own eyes, condescend to receive any thing at the hands of the barbarous Germans? Their pride, in fact, raised between the Reformation and themselves a barrier higher than the Alps. But the very nature of their mental culture was a still greater obstacle than the presumption of their hearts. Could men, who admired the elegance of a well cadenced sonnet more than the majestic simplicity of the Scriptures, be a propitious soil for the seed of God's word? A false civilization is, of all conditions of a nation, that which is most repugnant to the gospel."

Those who have read Roscoe's "Life and Pontificate of Leo X.," will greatly question the accuracy of this picture of Italian civilization. We shall prove in the sequel, that, both before and during the time of the Reformation, Italy did much more than Germany, to evidence her admiration "for the majestic simplicity of the Scriptures." At present we will barely remark, that the gist of D'Aubigné's theory consists in the assertion, that Italy was too enlightened, too refined in taste and social habits, too delicate in her own eyes, and consequently too proud and presumptuous to receive the new gospel; while Germany, being on the contrary, less enlightened, less refined, and more corrupt in doctrine and morals, was a more genial soil —just the one, in fact, which was most "ripe" for its reception, and most likely to foster its growth! We most cheerfully award to him the entire benefit of this novel and marvelous speculation on the most suitable means of disposing men's minds for the willing reception of gospel truth.

To confirm this singular theory still further, he thus accounts for the singular fact that Spain did not embrace Protestantism:

"Spain possessed, what Italy did not—a serious and noble people, whose religious mind has resisted even the stern trial of the eighteenth century, and of the revolution (French), and maintained itself to our own days. In every age, this people has had among its clergy men of piety and learning, and it was sufficiently remote from Rome to throw off without difficulty her yoke. There are few nations wherein one might more reasonably have hoped for a revival of that primitive Christianity, which Spain had probably received from St. Paul himself. And yet Spain did not then stand up among the nations. She was destined to be an example of that word of the divine wisdom, 'the first shall be last.'"

What a pity! We have little doubt ourselves, that these were precisely some of the principal reasons, why Spain did not stand up among the nations who revolted against Catholicity in the sixteenth century: and her having passed unscathed through this fiery ordeal of reckless innovation, may also serve to explain to us, how she was enabled "to resist even the stern trial of the eighteenth century, and of the revolution." Her people were too "serious and too noble," their mind was too "religious," and their clergy had too much "piety and learning," to allow them to be carried away by the novel vagaries of Protestantism.

Among the "various circumstances which conduced to the deplorable result"—of her remaining Catholic, D'Aubigné mentions her "remoteness from Germany," the *"heart"* of Europe —"an eager desire after riches" in the new world—the influence of her "powerful clergy"—and her military glory, which had just risen to its zenith, after the conquest of Grenada and the expulsion of the Moors. In reference to this last cause, he asks emphatically: "How could a people who had expelled Mohammed from their noble country, allow Luther to make way in it?"—This question is at least characteristic! Was there then, in the ideas of the serious and noble Spaniards, so little difference between Luther and Mohammed? And is our philosophic historian half inclined himself to think, that they were not so very far out in their logic!

"Few countries," he says, "seemed likely to be better disposed than France for the reception of the evangelical doctrines. Almost all the intellectual and spiritual life of the middle ages was concentrated in her. It might have been said, that the paths were everywhere trodden for a grand manifestation of the truth."—Perhaps this very preservation of the intellectual and spiritual life of the middle ages, was a principal reason why France continued Catholic. A little farther on, he continues: "The (French) people, of quick feeling, intelligent, and susceptible of generous emotions, were as open, or even more so than other nations, to the truth. It seemed as if the Reformation must be, among them, the birth which should crown the travail of several centuries. But the chariot of France, which seemed for so many generations to be advancing to the same goal, suddenly turned at the moment of the Reformation, and took a contrary direction. Such was the will of Him, who rules nations and their kings."—We greatly admire his pious resignation to the will of God! This sentiment may perhaps console him for his disappointment; "that the augury of ages was deceived," in regard to France. He adds, in the same pious strain: "Perhaps, if she had received the gospel, she might have become too powerful!"

He winds up his affecting Jeremiad over France with these and similar passages:

"France, after having been almost reformed, found herself, in the result, Roman Catholic. The sword of her princes, cast into the scale, caused it to incline in favor of Rome. Alas! another sword, that of the reformers themselves, insured the failure of the effort for reformation. The hands that had been accustomed to warlike weapons, ceased to be lifted up in prayer. It is by the blood of its confessors, not by that of its adversaries, that the gospel triumphs. Blood shed by its defenders, extinguishes and smothers it."—That is, the Reformation sought to establish itself in France by violence and by force, and it signally failed! Elsewhere, as we shall see, it was more successful in the employment of such carnal weapons. But Protestantism obtained sufficient foothold in France to do incredible mischief for a century and a half; and it sowed upon her beautiful soil the fatal seeds which, two centuries and a half later, produced the bitter fruits of anarchy, infidelity, and bloodshed, during the dreadful "reign of terror!"

Such is the theory of D'Aubigné in regard to what we may perhaps designate the philosophy of the Reformation; and we now proceed to its refutation;—which is no difficult task, as in fact it sufficiently refutes itself.

A historian trained in the older Roman Catholic approach but who lived well into what might be called the new era, P. H. GRISAR, S.J. (1845–1932) studied at the university at Innsbruck, Austria, and later became professor of Church History there. For many years he was one of the leading Austrian authorities on the Protestant and the Catholic Reformations. From his studies came *Martin Luther, His Life and Work* (originally published in German in 1926; English translation, 1930).*

► Tempest in State and Church

Powerful movements which, proclaiming an intellectual revolution and connected more or less intimately with the revival of the study of classical antiquity, pervaded the Western world since the fifteenth century, and presaged a new period in the history of mankind. This agitation was bound to react on young Luther.

The newly invented art of printing had at one stroke created a world-wide community of intellectual accomplishments and literary ideas, such as the Middle Ages had never dreamt of. By the exchange of the most diverse and far-reaching discoveries the nations came into closer proximity with one another.

The spirit of secular enterprise awakened as from a long sleep at the astounding discovery of new countries overseas with unsuspected treasures.

As a result of the increased facility of intellectual intercourse and of the development of scientific methods, criticism began to function with an efficiency greater than ever before in all departments of knowledge. Yielding to an ancient urge, the larger commonwealths made themselves increasingly independent of their former tutelage by the Church. They strove after liberty and the removal of that clerical influence whence they had largely derived their durability and internal prosperity in the

* Reprinted from P. H. Grisar, S.J., *Martin Luther, His Life and Work* (Westminster, Md.: The Newman Press, 1960), pp. 122–140. Footnotes omitted.

past. And in proportion as they struggled for autonomy, the opulent cities, the knightly demesnes and principalities, particularly in Germany, tried to throw off the fetters which hitherto had oppressed them, and to increase their power. In brief, we find everywhere a violent break with former restrictions, a determined advance of subjectivism at the expense of solidarity and the traditional order of the Middle Ages, but especially at the expense of the supremacy of the spiritual power of the Church, which thus far alone had preserved mankind from the dangers of individualism.

Influenced by the spirit of the Renaissance and the awakening of historical memories, the spirit of nationalism became more powerful than ever before in the life of peoples. The segregation of national ambitions became ever more pronounced, in spite of the increased solidarity of commerce. The Germans became more keenly conscious of being a unit which had a right to devolp along its own lines in opposition to the Latin nations. Luther very skillfully utilized this national spirit in his public conflict. He boldly aroused this spirit in the Germans, "his dear brethren," who had been reduced to servitude by the papacy, with a view to separate them from the universal Church. If the patriotic sentiment of the Germans had been kept within due bounds and had been animated by Christian ideals, it would have been a great good. Aside from other considerations, it might have led to a healthy competition with other civilized nations. In reality, however, it descended down to the individual principalities within the boundaries of Germany. The territorial rulers who concurred with Luther, promoted it to the advantage of their own power. In consequence, the empire increasingly became a cumbersome machine, and the authority of the emperor, the august head of the empire in virtue of his coronation by the pope, waned visibly, especially since the imperial reforms so warmly favored by Maximilian I (d. January 12, 1519) virtually failed and the immense and far-flung empire consolidated under Maximilian's successor, Charles V, almost completely absorbed the attention of that ruler to the detriment of his German subjects, not to speak of the impairment which the authority of this Catholic emperor experienced through Luther's widely-published attacks, made partly in the direct interest of his own ecclesiastical revolt and partly in the service of those petty German territorial rulers who were loyal to him and whose interests conflicted with those of the empire.

In course of time the German rulers obtained a certain ecclesiastical régime within their respective countries, and it came to pass that, at the close of the Middle Ages, besides the ecclesiastical princes, the secular princes were vested with extensive authority in the external administration of religious affairs. They derived this authority in part from the Roman See, which sought to protect and promote the interests of the Church by the aid of loyal Catholic rulers; in part they had acquired it as an inheritance from their forebears and maintained it against the passive or active opposition of the bishops.

This ecclesiastical régime exercised by territorial princes was a colossal danger when the religious struggles began in the sixteenth century.

True, some of the princes, e. g., the well-intentioned Duke George of Saxony and the dukes of Bavaria, employed their ecclesiastical power successfully in defense of the existing ecclesiastical conditions. Many others, however, especially Luther's territorial lord, the Elector of Saxony, constantly incited by him, and landgrave, Philip of Hesse, made of the ecclesiastical privileges they had gained a bulwark for the religious innovation. Thus the ecclesiastical authority of the territorial lords formed a convenient transition to the establishment of a Protestant ecclesiastical régime. Manifestly it was a double-edged sword which was thus wielded by the secular arm in the distribution of benefices, the temporal administration or partial disposition of church property, the control of innumerable ecclesiastical patronages and the superintendence of monasteries and ecclesiastical institutions. It happened that large territories were torn with ease from the faith and jurisdiction of the Church, as it were overnight. Even in principalities that remained Catholic, the reforms initiated by the Church authorities, *e. g.*, in the monasteries, were in many instances obstructed or interrupted by selfish rulers. And the acts of the reigning princes were repeated in the great free cities of the empire, and even in smaller cities, where the secular authorities had come into possession of similar powers.

It is remarkable how this tendency of transferring ecclesiastical functions and rights to secular rulers is noticeable in Luther's Commentary on the Epistle to the Romans, written at the time when he began to drift away from the Church. The young monk there asserts that the clergy are remiss in the performance of their duties concerning the administration of pious foundations. "As a matter of fact," he exclaims, "it were better and assuredly safer, if the temporal affairs of the clergy were placed under the control of the worldly authorities." The laity, he explains, are aware of the inefficiency of the clergy, and "the secular authorities fulfill their obligations better than our ecclesiastical rulers." It is a question whether he perceived the far-reaching import of his words as a kind of prelude to the coming secularization.

In any event, Luther was aware of the opposition existing between the secular powers, and even between the common laity, and the clergy, which smouldered in many places at that time. A certain aversion and hostility toward the entire clergy, commencing with the curia and the episcopate, and extending to the lower secular clergy and the monks, had become widely prevalent and was fomented by the secular authorities. In virtue of the pious donations that had accumulated in the course of centuries, the Church had become too wealthy. Thus, in the diocese of Worms, about three-fourths of all property belonged to ecclesiastical proprietors. Everywhere the Church possessed a plenitude of privileges which provoked envy, as, for illustration, in the judicial forum, in her exemption from taxation, and in the honors bestowed upon her. Jealousy and envy engendered hatred and contentions in many places. True, an immense share of the income of the Church constantly flowed to charitable institutions; other sums were allotted with papal sanction to, or else arbitrarily appropriated by, the secular authorities to cover particular needs. Large sums were remitted to the Roman curia in the form of ordinary or extraordinary taxes. The wealth of the Church was alluring, and the large subsidies from Germany to Rome especially were a constant occasion for complaint.

The payments to the papal treasury had, as a matter of fact, become too onerous. The urgent requirements of the administration of the universal Church, especially since the exile of the popes at Avignon, had resulted in constantly increasing imposts levied on the faithful in the various countries for the benefit of Rome. The *annates,* the *servitia* and other taxes, and the revenues derived from indulgences had constantly increased. In Germany complaints were rife that the material resources of the country were too heavily assessed. The so-called *"courtesans,"* i. e., benefice-hunters provided with Roman documents entitling them to certain benefices, by their avaricious practices helped to render the papal curia still more odious.

At the commencement of his controversy Luther assiduously collected every unfavorable detail concerning the financial practices of the curia, so as to paint a collective picture of them for propaganda purposes. In this task he was assisted by a former official of the Roman curia who had come to Wittenberg. True and exaggerated reports of the pomp displayed at the court of Rome and of the papal expenditures for secular purposes reacted upon the discontented like oil poured into a fire.

A historical expression of this bitter feeling is furnished by the so-called *Gravamina,* official lists of complaints submitted to successive diets by the princes and estates against the excessive burdens and the inequality of rights. In many respects these complaints met with the approval of men who were sincerely attached to the Church, such as Dr. Eck. Similarly the cities had their *Gravamina* against the bishops, the citizens and town councilors against the chapters and the other clergy. The spiritual principalities repeatedly experienced a clash of arms as a result of the quarrels pertaining to jurisdiction or possession.

In this way it appeared—and the more recent researches concerning local conditions confirm the impression—that one reason for the great defection was antagonism to the papal government and to the clergy, originating in material interests. The aversion to Rome was all the more dangerous because it was shared by a large number of the clergy, oppressed by taxes. These were clouds that heralded an approaching storm. Nevertheless, the reform for which many serious-minded churchmen clamored was not excluded, but merely delayed. The existing discontent did not engender a desire for a new religion, and the Catholic dogmas remained sacred. But when Luther proclaimed his new doctrines, which implied the destruction of ecclesiastical unity, the existing discontent accelerated the revolution.

Abuses in the Life of the Clergy

When Cardinal Nicholas of Cusa (d. 1462), a man who has merited the gratitude of Germany, proclaimed his programme of reforms, he indicated with complete frankness the reasons for the corruption of the ecclesiastical system. They were: the admission of many unworthy candidates to the clerical state, sacerdotal concubinage, the accumulation of benefices, and simony. Towards the end of the fifteenth century complaints had multiplied against immorality among the clergy. "The numerous decrees of bishops and synods do not admit of a doubt but that a large part of the German clergy flagrantly transgressed the law of celibacy." A recommendation made to the dukes of Bavaria in 1447, voicing the opinion of many friends and sponsors of a sound reform, declared that the work of reformation had to begin with the improvement of the morals of the clergy, for here was the root of all evils in the Church. True there were districts where the clergy was irreproachable and praiseworthy, *e. g.,* the Rhineland, Slesvig-Holstein, and the Allgäu. But in Saxony, the home of Luther, and in Franconia and Bavaria, there were reports of many and grave abuses. A work entitled *De Ruina Ecclesiae,* formerly ascribed to Nicholas of Clémanges, says that at the beginning of the fifteenth century there were bishops who, for a money consideration, permitted their priests to live in concubinage, and Hefele in his *Konziliengeschichte* adduces a number of synodal decrees which prohibited bishops to accept money or gifts in consideration of their tolerating or ignoring the practice of concubinage.

In addition to living in concubinage, many of the better situated clergy were steeped in luxury and presumptuous arrogance, thus repelling the people, and especially the middle class, which was conscious of its own self-sufficiency.

In connection with the unduly multiplied small religious foundations without clergy, the number of clergymen had increased to such an extent that their very number suggests the idea that many of them had no genuine vocation to the clerical state, and that lack of work constituted a moral danger for many. Thus, at the end of the fifteenth century, two churches in Breslau had 236 "altarists," whose only service consisted in saying Mass at altars erected by pious donations and endowed with petty benefices. Besides saying Mass daily, these "altarists," of whom there was a vast multitude

throughout the country, had but one obligation, namely, to recite the Breviary. In 1480 there were 14 "altarists" and 60 vicars, besides 14 canons, stationed at the cathedral of Meissen. In Strasburg the minster boasted 36 canonries, St. Thomas Church 20, old St. Peter's 17, new St. Peter's 15, All Saints 12. The number of canonries was augmented by numerous foundations for vicars and "summissaries," so called because they celebrated high Mass in place of the canons. There were no less than 63 "summissaries" at the minster of Strasburg, not to mention 38 chaplains. John Agricola reports—although only on the strength of an *on dit* ("it is alleged")— that there were 5,000 priests and monks at Cologne; on another occasion he estimates the number of monks and nuns in that city alone at 5,000. It is certain that the "German Rome" on the Rhine at that time had 11 foundations, 19 parish churches, more than 100 chapels, 22 cloisters, 12 hospitals, and 76 religious convents.

The bishop of Chiemsee traces the corruption of the clergy principally to the fact that the spiritual and temporal rulers abused the right of patronage, both by their appointments and their arbitrary interference. This opinion is shared by Geiler of Kaysersberg, who blames the laity, in particular the patrons among the nobility, for the deplorable condition of the parishes and asserts that illiterate, malicious, and depraved individuals were engaged in lieu of the good and honorable.

In contrast with "the higher clergy, who reveled in wealth and luxury," the condition of the lower clergy in no wise corresponded to the dignity of their state. "Beyond the tithes and stole-fees, which were quite precarious, they had no stipends, so that poverty, and at times avarice, constrained them to gain their livelihood in a manner which exposed them to public contempt. 'There can be no doubt that a very large portion of the lower clergy had become unfaithful to the ideal of their state, so much so that one is justified in speaking of a clerical proletariat both in the higher sense, as well as in the ordinary and literal sense.' This clerical proletariat was prepared to join any movement which promised to abet its lower impulses."

The condition created by the all too frequent incorporation of parishes with monasteries was deplorable. Where many parishes were incorporated with one monastery, incompetent pastors were frequently sent, there was no supervision, and the care of souls declined.

One of the chief causes of the decline of the higher clergy and the episcopate was the interference of the secular authorities and worldly-minded noblemen in church affairs.

Not only were spiritual prerogatives frequently usurped by the princes and lesser authorities, but large numbers of cathedral benefices and diocesan sees were arbitrarily conferred on noblemen and princely scions, so that the most influential offices were occupied in many places by individuals who were unworthy and without a proper vocation. "When the storm broke loose at the end of the second decade of the sixteenth century, the following archdioceses and dioceses were administered by sons of princes: Bremen, Freising, Halberstadt, Hildesheim, Magdeburg, Mayence, Merseburg, Metz, Minden, Münster, Naumburg, Osnabrück, Paderborn, Passau, Ratisbon, Spires, Verden, and Verdun." As a rule, the bishops who came from

princely houses were dependent upon their relatives and were drawn into secular and courtly activities, even if their education had not radically repressed their ecclesiastical sense, as, for instance, in the case of the powerful archbishop of Mayence, Albrecht of Brandenburg.

An additional evil was the concentration of prominent episcopal sees. "The archbishop of Bremen was also bishop of Verden, the bishop of Osnabrück was also bishop of Paderborn, the archbishop of Mayence was also archbishop of Magdeburg and bishop of Halberstadt. George, palsgrave of the Rhine and duke of Bavaria, was provost of the cathedral of Mayence when but thirteen and successively became vicar capitular of Cologne and Treves, provost of the foundation of St. Donatian at Bruges, incumbent of the parishes of Hochheim and Lorch on the Rhine, and, lastly, in 1513, bishop of Spires. By special privilege of Pope Leo X, conferred under date of June 22, 1513, he, a sincere and pious man, was given possession of all these benefices in addition to the bishopric of Spires." "The higher clergy," laments a contemporary in view of the worldly bishops, "are chiefly to blame for the wretched condition of the parishes. They appoint unfit persons to administer parishes, whilst they themselves collect the tithes. Many endeavor to concentrate as many benefices as possible in their own hands, without satisfying the obligations attached to them, and dissipate the ecclesiastical revenues in luxurious expenditures lavished on servants, pages, dogs, and horses. One endeavors to outdo the other in ostentation and luxury." The decline and indolence of the episcopate furnishes one of the **most important explanations of** the rapid defection from the ancient Church after Luther had set the ball a-rolling.

The religious tragedy of the sixteenth century is a perfectly insoluble riddle except on the assumption that there was great corruption within the Church. It is, however, a mistake to think that the abuses were engendered by the nature of the Church, and that, therefore, her doctrines and her hierarchy had necessarily to be abandoned. Her exterior life, it is true, was greatly disfigured; yet there was vitality in her soul and her salutary powers were unbroken. Placed in the midst of mankind and exposed to the frailties of the world in her human element, the Church, as the preceding centuries of her existence show, is subject to periods of decline in her exterior manifestation, without, however, being deprived of the hope of seeing her interior light shine forth anew and her deformity vanish in God's appointed time. She celebrated such a renaissance after the decline of the spiritual life in the eleventh century, in consequence of the warfare which the great pope Gregory VII and his successors waged upon the tyranny of the secular rulers and the numerous infractions of clerical celibacy. She experienced a similar rejuvenation in the sixteenth century, after the anti-ecclesiastical elements had drained off into the new ecclesiastical system, to which they had been attracted by the offer of emancipation from the commandments of the Church.

Brighter Phases

For the rest there are many bright spots in the ecclesisatical conditions of pre-Lutheran Germany. This is true especially of the life of the common people, which went on in conformity with the old spirit, nay, even became more truly religious despite all obstacles. It is true also of the various religious orders, such as the Francisans and Dominicans, as well as of many portions of the secular clergy. A modern Protestant historian writes: "We hear of grave defects. . . . And again we hear of so many monasteries imbued with seriousness and character, of so many diligent efforts made for the improvement of the parochial clergy, of such eager solicitude for the faithful, of such fruitful fostering of studies within the Church, that we hesitate to assume that vice and loathsomeness ruled absolutely. We shall be compelled to establish the fact that gratifying and deplorable things are to be found side by side; that there are some phenomena which are depressing in the highest degree, but many others which are elevating; and that the relationship which they bore to one another was such as no one may venture to describe in numbers."

From the very beginning of his internal defection from the dogmatic teaching of the Church, Luther had no appreciation of these elevating and gratifying conditions. His preconceived delineation of affairs does not constitute an objection to the brighter pages which ought to be adduced.

As an illustration: in his commentary on the Epistle to the Romans, where he expresses the thought that "the temporalities of the clergy ought to be administered by the secular authorities," he outdoes himself in unduly generalized complaints against the clergy. Thus he says: What Paul demanded of the servants of the Church, is "done by no one at the present day. They are priests only in appearance. . . . Where is there one who does the will of the Founder? . . . The laity are beginning to

SAMBROSE LUTHERAN COLLEGE LIBRARY

penetrate the mysteries of our iniquity (*mysteria iniquitatis*). . . . Beyond proceeding against such as violate their liberties, possessions, and rights, the ecclesiastical authorities know naught else but pomp, ambition, unchastity, and contentiousness." They are one and all "whitened sepulchres."

Such exaggerated invectives are associated in his earliest literary productions and letters with those fantastic descriptions which we were constrained to adduce on previous pages.

Thus, in 1516, he wrote to Spalatin to dissuade the Elector of Saxony from promoting Staupitz to a bishopric: He who becomes a bishop in these days falls into the most evil company; all the wickedness of Greece, Rome, and Sodom were to be found in the bishops. A pastor of souls was regarded as quite exemplary if he merely pushed his worldly business, and prepared for himself an insatiable hell with his riches.

Everywhere he perceived only dark gloom, because he discovered that the Gospel as he understood it was everywhere forgotten; for, where the "word of truth" does not reign, there can be only "dark iniquity." "The whole world," he exclaims as early as 1515, or in the period immediately succeeding, "the whole world is full of, yea, deluged with, the filth of false doctrine." Hence, it is not astonishing that there is prevalent in Christendom "so much dissension, anger, covetousness, pride, disobedience, vice, and intemperance, in consequence of which charity has grown completely cold, faith has become extinguished, and hope has vanished." etc.

In view of these unrestrained and exaggerated effusions on the decline of the Church, which pervade his whole life and are expanded into a condemnation of all previous ages as the kingdom of Antichrist, it is well to observe that they are inspired mainly by his new dogmatic and pseudomystical views. They are anything but historical and balanced judgments, and one can but marvel at the thought that they have influenced the evaluation of the Middle Ages for so long a time among Protestant scholars. To-day, however, well informed Protestant writers are beginning to speak differently of Luther's unjustified and impassioned verdicts.

It is conceded that his discourses were based on "a one-sided and distorted view" of things, and that he painted the history of the Middle Ages, directed by the popes, as "a dark night."

With respect to medieval theology, we read that it is necessary to repudiate resolutely "the caricature we meet with in the writings of the reformers" and "the misunderstandings to which they gave rise."

A historian of the Reformation, writing in 1910, conceded that the history of the close of the Middle Ages was "an almost unknown terrain up to a few years ago;" "the later Middle Ages seemed to be useful only to serve as a foil for the story of the reformers, whose dazzling colors, when superimposed on a gray background, shone forth with greater brilliancy;" only since Janssen has "a more intensive study of the close of the Middle Ages" been made, and it has been discovered that "the Church had not yet lost its influence over souls." "An increasing acquaintance with the Bible toward the end of the Middle Ages must be admitted" and "preaching in the vernacular was not neglected to the extent frequently assumed."

The first volume of Janssen's History, despite the necessary modifications made in later editions, clearly reveals that there was a striking revival in many spheres of ecclesiastical life before Luther. Popular religious literature flourished to a certain extent under the fostering care of the new art of printing. It is impossible to assume that such excellent and frequently reprinted works

CAMROSE LUTHERAN COLLEGE
LIBRARY

as *Der Schatzbehälter des Heils* (The Treasure Trove of Salvation), *Das Seelenwurzgärtlein* (The Little Aromatic Garden of the Soul), *Der Christenspiegel* (The Mirror for Christians), *Der Seelenführer* (The Spiritual Guide of the Soul), etc., should not have awakened a response in the morals of the people and the general sentiment of the age. Booklets on penance and confession, treatises on matrimony, books on death, pictorial catechisms with instructive illustrations, explanations of the faith and the current prayers, printed tables with the commandments of God and a catalogue of domestic duties, as well as many similar publications were widely disseminated among the people. Excellent books of sermons were found in the hands of the clergy. The classic work of Thomas à Kempis went through no less than fifty-nine editions in several languages before the year 1500. The admirable pedagogical writings of Jacob Wimpfeling, who was styled the "teacher of Germany," were published in thirty different editions within twenty-five years. Among the products of the press the Bible ranked supreme. The first artistic work from the press of Koberger (in Nuremberg) was the splendid German Bible of 1483, which Michael Wohlgemut had oramented with more than a hundred woodcuts. It was entitled "the most excellent work of the entire Sacred Scripture . . . according to correct vernacular German, with beautiful illustrations."

The making of religious woodcuts and copper-plate engravings flourished as perhaps never before. Sculptures and paintings vied with one another in fervor, depth of thought, and beauty of execution. Like all the artistic products of that day, they are permeated by tenderness and sincere piety. This phase of art production is a favorable mirror of the life of the people.

In the town-church of Wittenberg, sculpture has bequeathed to us two splendid models in the richly ornamented baptismal font of 1457, a creation of Herman Vischer, and in the artistically constructed pulpit of the Luther Hall, in which Luther is said to have preached frequently. The principal portal of the church is still adorned with figures sculptured in the lovely style in vogue at the close of the Middle Ages. In the center the enthroned Madonna with her Child looks down upon and invites the worshipers. Sculptures such as this attractive group of saints reveal as clearly as the popular books just mentioned, how far the people were removed from regarding religion as a source of horror and fear, as Luther will have it. In life as well as in art, they, on the contrary, harmoniously combined a loving trust in Jesus, the Divine Lord, and confidence in the intercession of His servants, the Saints, grouped around Mary, with the gravity of the idea of the eternal Judge, who appears on the outside of the town-church of Wittenberg, a large statue set in the wall. The majestic figure, with a sword protruding from the mouth, in compliance with the Bible, inspires the beholder with a sense of awe. It is not impossible that Luther's morbid fear of God's judgment attached itself to such pictures, for the healthy piety of the Middle Ages was wont to place them beside the monuments of its confidence and childlike hope of salvation, as a counterpoise to the spirit of levity.

Ecclesistical architecture, finally, constituted a splendid field of artistic endeavor. It was the center of all art. There is scarcely another age in the history of architecture like the century from 1420 to 1520, in which town and country witnessed the erection of so many houses of worship—most of them still in existence—constructed in the devotional and joyful style of the late Gothic. The confraternity of the German builders was the chief bearer of this great movement, and it was one of the most popular institutions of the time. The large sums which the faithful contributed towards the erection of these often marvelous structures, attest the charity and the idealism that actuated the soul of the nation.

In his journey to Rome, which took him through the heart of Germany, Luther had ample opportunities of seeing and admiring the artistic creations of architecture, sculpture, and painting, some of which are still extant, whilst others have perished. But the monk of Wittenberg had no taste for such things. There is not a sentence of his writings or addresses which betrays any appreciation of the mighty impetus of ecclesiastical life represented by the works of art in churches and monasteries. In fact, neither his tongue nor his pen reveals any genuine appreciation of art. He lived a secluded life in his own narrow world, which fact explains the rigor of many of his judgments.

Preponderance of Dangerous Elements

Having depicted the favorable aspects of the age, it is necessary once more to revert to its shadows. They must have constituted a source of grave danger to the Church, to judge of certain writings of unbiased and noble-minded contemporaries, such as the indictment of the bishop of Chiemsee, Berthold Pirstinger, published in 1519 under the title, *Onus*

Ecclesiae, a phrase borrowed from the Apocalypse. True, in spite of the "burdens" imposed upon the Church he hoped for an internal restoration of the same, based on the unchangeable foundation of the faith. He mournfully addresses Christ as follows: "Grant that the Church may be reformed, which has been redeemed by Thy blood, and is now, through our fault, near destruction!" After a dismal description of existing conditions, he says that the "episcopate is now given up to worldly possessions, sordid cares, tempestuous feuds, worldly sovereignty." He complains that "the prescribed provincial and diocesan synods are not held"; that the shepherds of the Church do not remain at their posts, although they exact heavy tributes; and that the conduct of the clergy and the laity had become demoralized, and so on.

Trithemius, Wimpfeling, Brant, Geiler von Kaysersberg, and Dr. John Eck, joined in the lament of the Bishop of Chiemsee.

"Of the Lamentation of the Church" (*De Planctu Ecclesiae*) was the title of a work which had enjoyed quite a wide circulation before Luther's day. It was reprinted at Ulm in 1474, and again at Lyons in 1517. It was originally composed against the faults of the papacy during the Avignon period, by the Franciscan Alvarez Pelayo, a man of strict morality and whole-heartedly devoted to the Church. The new reprints of this work addressed the contemporaries of Luther in the severe language of Pelayo on the persecution of the Church by those who were instituted as her protectors. In another censorious composition, *De Squaloribus Curiae*, many justifiable complaints were registered side by side with unfounded reproaches. The work entitled *De Ruina Ecclesiae* gained new importance at the end of the fifteenth century.

Luther's mental depression and distorted notions cannot be traced to this kind of literature. Yet it is known from reliable sources that he read other books of a similar tenor, such as the elegant works of the pious Italian poet Mantuanus, who indignantly describes the moral corruption of his country, extending to the highest ecclesiastical dignitaries at Rome. In the writings of the new humanists he found an echo, alloyed with bitter contempt, of what he himself had heard at Rome, fortified by all the complaints of the age against the clergy and the monks. We know that he did not approve their attitude, in so far as it antagonized religion, nor was he himself a humanist; but humanism with its critical activity, as developed everywhere, especially in Germany under the influence of Erasmus, proved to be a great help to him in his revolt against the Church authorities.

The papacy gradually came to regret the favor which it had extended to, and the hopes it had placed in, the nascent humanism in Rome and Italy. Among the German Humanists, Conrad Mutianus of Gotha (d. 1526) was the chief promoter of the anti-ecclesiastical móve-ment. He was a man who had gone so far as to abandon Christianity for a time. From this group originated the "Epistolae Obscurorum Virorum," a clever and biting satyre on monks, scholastics, and friends of the papal curia. Crotus Rubeanus, its principal author, had gathered a circle of younger Humanists about him at an earlier stage of his career, among them Eobanus Hessus, Peter and Henry Eberbach, John Lang, Spalatin for a time, and other talented

men desirous of innovation. Erfurt became the headquarters of this group, which was very clamorous in prose and verse.

Justus Jonas also lived at Erfurt. He was a Humanist who later associated himself for life with Luther. While yet a student of law in 1506, he became affiliated with the Humanistic circles of that city. He called Erasmus his "father in Christ" and, in company with Casper Schalbe, made a pilgrimage to him in the Netherlands. In the same year Jonas, who was a priest and canon of St. Severus, became rector of the University of Erfurt, an event which greatly fortified the position of the neo-Humanists. The Leipsic disputation and the letters of Luther aroused his enthusiasm. When Luther journeyed to the diet of Worms, in 1521, Jonas set out to meet him at Weimar, accompanied him to Worms, and subsequently was called to Wittenberg as provost of the castle-church and professor of canon law. Here, as early as 1521, having obtained his doctorate, Justus Jonas taught theology in concordance with the ideas of Luther. By his intimate attachment to Luther he gained the praise and friendship of such a questionable man as Ulrich von Hutten.

Ulrich von Hutten, humanist and knight, took an active part in the literary feud of Reuchlin against the "Obscurantists." In 1517 he circulated the treatise of Laurentius Valla, an Italian, against the so-called Donation of Constantine, with a view of making a breach in the system of the Roman hierarchy and in a malicious libel ridiculed the conduct of the celebrated theologian Cajetan at the diet of Augsburg. In 1519 he dedicated to his patron, Archbishop Albrecht of Mayence, a work on a cure for syphilis which he had taken with temporary success. He had contracted this disease in consequence of his dissolute life. Wielding a pen skilled in polemics this adventurous Humanist launched his attacks on Rome, thereby becoming the pathfinder of religious schism. Towards his offers of forcible support, Luther prudently assumed a reserved attitude, preferring the protection of his prince to the mailed fist of the revolutionary. Politically, too, Hutten was a revolutionist. Like his friend Franz von Sickingen, he was inspired by the ideal of a powerful and independent knighthood. He fought with Sickingen in the army of the Swabian League when it undertook the expulsion of Duke Ulrich of Württemberg. Afterwards he lived in the Ebernburg, Sickingen's castle in the Palatinate, the so-called "Inn of Justice." Here he devoted himself to the composition of popular and witty writings directed against the clergy and the princes.

The highly revered prince of the Humanists was Erasmus of Rotterdam, at one time an Augustinian canon of Emaus at Gouda, a scholar of prodigious learning and an epoch-making critic, whose ambition it was, not only to introduce a new Humanistic form of speech into ecclesiastical science, but also to reconstruct theology along Humanistic lines, thereby exposing its dogmas to the danger of extinction. While he wished to remain loyal to the Church, his caustic and frequently derisive criticism of things ecclesiastical, Scholasticism, monasticism, and the hierarchy, so influenced the minds of his idolizing followers, both learned and illiterate, as to render the greatest assistance to the work of Luther. His opponents coined the phrase that his writings contained the egg which Luther hatched. At all events, his initial sympathy for Luther was one of the causes that induced almost the entire powerful and wide-spread neo-Humanistic party to join the reform movement of Wittenberg, until finally, about 1524, when it had been clearly demonstrated that the religious struggles were redounding to the disadvantage of the sciences, a reaction set in and Erasmus began to write against Luther.

The great services which Erasmus rendered in behalf of the text of Sacred Scripture and his excellent editions of the writings of the Fathers, remained undisputed and were acknowledged even by his adversaries. In 1516 he issued his first edition of the Greek New Testament, accompanied by a translation into classical Latin, which was followed by his Biblical "Paraphrases." In 1521 he took up his abode near the printing-presses of Basle, whence, in 1529, the disturbances caused by the new religion compelled him to remove to Freiburg in Breisgau. Everywhere in his solitary greatness he was an oracle of the learned. But his character was disfigured by weakness of conviction and pronounced self-conceit. He lacked the power of leadership, such as that trying and dangerous epoch demanded, especially since his unfavorable characteristics were also impressed upon his Humanistic admirers.

Besides Humanism, there were in those critical decades certain other factors which constrain us to speak of a preponderance of imminent dangers.

The minds of men had not yet completely divested themselves of the consequences of the conciliar theories begotten in the unhappy period of the Council of Basle, and of the schisms that preceded it, with its two anti-popes in addition to the one true pope. Here and there the Hussite theories, which had taken deep root in Bohemia, made themselves felt in Germany. A worldly spirit and an unbridled desire for wealth, which the newly inaugurated international commerce and the attractive trade-routes to distant countries aroused in the upper classes of society, were evidenced by the growing evil of usury, against which Luther took a stand in two sermons delivered in 1519 and 1520, though he lacked "an adequate comprehension of the existing conditions." In the lower strata of society, especially among the peasant class, the long-nurtured discontent with oppressive conditions began here and there to issue in unrest and revolt. Lingering politico-social ideas of Hussitism coöperated in this respect with aspirations after a higher standard of living, awakened by the influx of wealth. The unrest was increased by opposition to the introduction into Germany, about 1520, of the Christian-Roman system of jurisprudence, interspersed with Germanic principles. A fanatical preacher of social revolution in favor of the lower classes was the prophet Hans Böhm, a piper of Niklashausen in the Tauber valley. The "Bundschuh"—*i. e.*, the strapped shoe commonly worn by peasants—was the symbol of revolts which broke out in many places, first in 1486, then in 1491 and 1492, but especially in 1513 and 1514, and again in 1517. The social revolution of 1525, with the new Gospel of the "liberty of the Christian man" as its background, was thus gradually prepared.

Only a man of superhuman powers could have banished the threatening dangers of the age in the name of religion and an amelioration of the traditional social order. Who can tell what course events might have taken if at that time saintly men had inspired the people with a reviving spiritual vigor, repeating the example of ancient leaders in reshaping their age? But the teacher of Wittenberg, who took it upon himself to direct the course of events, was no such leader, as the sequel showed.

Many hailed the generous young emperor, Charles V, as the leader who would conduct men out of the religious and social crisis. This young ruler of a world-wide monarchy was animated by the best of intentions. In all sincerity he, as emperor-elect, rendered the customary oath of fealty to the Church on the occasion of his coronation, before he was anointed by the archbishop of Cologne and girded with the "sword of Charles the Great." The oath he took bound him "to preserve and defend in every way the Holy Catholic Faith, as handed down," and "at all times to render due submission, respect, and fealty to the Roman Pontiff, the Holy Father and Lord in Christ, and to the Holy Roman Church." During a life replete with wars and disappointments, Charles honestly endeavored to perform in his beloved Germany the duties which he had assumed; but the religious schism overwhelmed him and finally paralyzed the vigor and determination with which he had begun his career despite constant diversions.

The papacy, too, after Leo X, manifested many hopeful traits of energy and efforts at reform, especially in the brief pontificate of Adrian VI; but there was missing that towering personality on the pontifical throne which might have averted the catostrophe. It was necessary that the idea of a true, distinct from a false, reform of the Church should make its way gradually at Rome and in Germany, until it triumphed at the great Council of Trent in Charles Borromeo and Pope St. Pius V, after the Church had sustained immense losses. But no matter what the popes of Luther's day might have done in the interest of reform, in Luther's eyes their endeavors would have been futile; for he was firmly convinced that they had become rulers of the kingdom of Antichrist.

HUGH ROSS WILLIAMSON (b. 1901), the son of
a clergyman of the Church of England, began his
career as a journalist on the staff of the *Yorkshire Post*,
later becoming editor of *The Bookman* and of the
Strand Magazine. He took orders in the Church of
England, but in 1955 left to become a Roman Catholic
priest. Since 1932 he has written voluminously. Many
of his works are in the field of history or biography:
James I (1936); *George Villiers, Duke of Buckingham*
(1940); *The Gunpowder Plot* (1951); *James, by the
Grace of God* (1955) and many others, all of which
reflect changes in his point of view. In 1955 *The
Beginnings of the English Reformation* set forth
emphatically an interpretation of the Reformation
rather different from that of Protestant historians.*

The English Reformation:
An Expression of Greed

The Reformation has been well defined as a sixteenth-century movement which, while ostensibly directed towards the spiritual renewal of the Church, was in fact a revolt against it and led to the abandonment by the Reformers of essential Christian doctrines. The causes of the Reformation, like those of the fall of the Roman Empire or the outbreak of the French Revolution, provide endless opportunities for neat theses and provoke interminable, if inconclusive, academic arguments.

Catholic historians have themselves admitted and even emphasized that among these causes were the worldliness of many high ecclesiastics, striving for political power and privilege, and, in particular, the appalling state, in this respect, of the Papal Curia; the idleness, superstition, ignorance and indifference of many Christians, including the religious as well as the secular priests; the diminution of the prestige of Holy See by the Babylonish Captivity and the Great Schism, which accustomed men, during the fourteenth and fifteen centuries, to underestimate, if not wholly to ignore, the universal and unique character of the Papacy; the organizational concentration of administrative affairs at Rome, with the resultant delay and expense, which exasperated increasingly powerful national interests; and the impact of Renaissance humanism on Christendom in general and the Papacy in

---

* From *The Beginnings of the English Reformation* by Hugh Ross Williamson. © Copyright 1957 by Sheed & Ward, Inc. Pp. 9–21.

particular. This case has been vividly stated by Karl Adam in the opening pages of *The Roots of the Reformation. . . .*

Yet, true though these things are, there is another aspect of the truth which must be kept in mind if the perspective is not to become distorted and history "read backwards" with an undue deference to later Protestant propaganda. The Church, as far as the human element goes, has always needed reform, though it has seldom fallen to the level which St. Paul denounced in the apostolic church at Corinth; the proportion of traitors in the Christian ranks has probably remained in the apostolic ratio of one in twelve and the collective Judas through the ages has been no less active than the individual "son of perdition" was; and the "anti-clericalism" which is at all levels the lever for discontent is a persistent phenomenon, arising from the nature of society, and is not even confined to Christianity. To be "agin" the powers that be—ecclesiastical, or political, or even cultural—is a universal human tendency; elements both unhealthy and healthy are complicatedly combined in it, and although this study affords neither scope nor occasion for analysing its significance, it can at least be said that anti-clericalism in the ordinary sense is, in part at any rate, simply one particular manifestation of it.

The decisive factor, at any point in history, is not conditions but men's reaction to those conditions. The state of affairs, moral, political, ecclesiastical and social, against which St. Theresa of Avila had to struggle in her efforts for reform was no different from those which faced Luther; but she is one of the greatest of saints and he one of the most dangerous of heresiarchs precisely because she saw

and accepted (which he did not) the ultimate irrelevance of those conditions to the central truth that, whatever the failings of the human element, the Church is the mystical body of Christ. To St. Catherine of Siena, the Babylonish Captivity which oppressed her spirit with its horror, was not primarily a subject for theological denunciations but an opportunity to fetch the Pope back from Avignon. And in England it was St. John Fisher who said: "If the Pope will not reform the Curia God will find the means to do it for him" and St. Thomas More who wrote *Utopia*. Always the true reformers are the great saints and the measure of the Church's perennial need for reformation is their sanctity and their vision.

Thus, in England, the Protestant triumph was made possible by the failure of Tudor Catholics to fulfil their faith. Three sentences will serve for epitome. St. John Fisher said of his fellow bishops: "The fort is betrayed even of them which should have defended it." St. Thomas More described the English priests as "a weak clergy lacking grace constantly to stand to their learning". And for the laity the Duke of Bedford may be spokesman when he refused to return the plundered property of the Church but threw his rosary into the fire saying that, much as he loved it, he loved his "sweet Abbey of Woburn" more.

The Reformation in England was made possible by the existence of fear, weakness and self-seeking in the very places where, above all, one might have expected courage, strength and loyalty. No estimate of it which denies or minimizes this can pretend to accuracy. But, having admitted it, one must admit also that the men of the time had the excuse that originally the religious issue was not as clear-cut as it became later or as it appears to posterity. For there was no immediate doctrinal cleavage. The Reformation in England differs radically from that in Germany. Henry VIII was no Luther. The divorce of the queen had no connection with the theses at Wittenberg. The Church in England was not corrupt, though it was certainly in need of reorganization and, as far as "reform" was genuine, it was a Catholic organizational reform, as for instance in the matter of Wolsey's attitude to small, under-staffed monasteries. Heresy, though it existed, was small in numbers and practically negligible in influence and there was no popular discontent to fan it. Not for twenty years after the beginning of the Reformation were Protestant doctrines officially adopted and then they had to be forced on the people by German mercenaries after popular uprisings in fourteen counties. "The one definite thing which can be said about the Reformation in England," writes Sir Frederick Powicke, "is that it was an Act of State." From this unassailable premiss, which to-day is admitted freely by non-Catholic historians, all the rest proceeds as an inexorable logical necessity. The later doctrinal change was merely an ideological justification for the political and economic revolution which that Act of State deliberately initiated. Practice preceded principles.

A foreign visitor to England at the beginning of the sixteenth century noted that the English were extremely pious. "They all attend Mass every day," he wrote, "and say many *Paternosters* in public. The women carry long rosaries in their hands and any who can read take the Office of Our Lady with them and with some companion recite it in church verse by verse, in a low voice, after the manner of churchmen. On Sunday they always hear Mass in their parish church and give liberal alms." They understood the Faith they practised. The circulation of devotional and instructional books among the population of three million may be gauged by the fact that, in the holocaust of Catholic learning and piety which was part of the Reformers' policy, a quarter of a million liturgical books alone were destroyed. The splendour of the shrines of the saints in England was one of the marvels of Europe, as pilgrimages to them were part of the social life of the land. The bare framework of chantries still to be seen in English cathedrals and churches —a proportion only of the chantries (which were also the schools) of the land —still bears witness to the piety of those who left endowments for Masses for souls.

No one can seriously contend that these people passionately believed that the doctrine of purgatory, the veneration paid to relics, the invocation of saints and prayers for the dead were "fond things vainly invented" and "repugnant to the word of God", as they were officially forced to believe after the State had enriched itself by tens of millions of pounds by destroying the shrines of the saints and stealing their treasures, and by pillaging the chantries and confiscating their endowments. On the contrary, the belief in the doctrines had so manifested itself in the whole texture of the nation's life and thought that only the blindest can fail to see why the State had to attempt to justify, by the importation of a new and convenient theology, a revolution accurately described by a Protestant historian as "a sweeping redistribution of wealth, carried out by an unscrupulous minority, using the weapons of violence, intimidation and fraud, and succeeded by an orgy of interested misgovernment on the part of its principal beneficiaries."[1]

This inverted relation of theory to practice is clear enough now. And, once the issue was stated in theological terms, it became clear enough then, as the succession of martyrs bears witness. But at the beginning of it all, in the early 1530's, even good and wise men failed to see that, in matters apparently concerned with such technicalities as the extent of the royal jurisdiction, the payment of ecclesiastical dues and the reorganization of monastic houses, what was at

stake was the Catholic Faith itself. It took, literally, a saint to see it in all its implications. And from among the clergy, St. John Fisher and, from among the laity, St. Thomas More, saw it and died for the vision.

But to the ordinary man and woman, lay or religious, the outward appearance of the Church in relation to the Holy See was, as Henry VII had left it and as Henry VIII preserved it in the early years of the reign, calm and even conventional. At the opening of the sixteenth century, in 1501, Henry VII had admitted the papal nuncio who had come to sell indulgences for the Pope's cherished project of a crusade against the Turks (the indulgences were for the faithful who had been unable to attend the previous year's Jubilee in Rome) and the king forwarded the whole of the proceeds—£4,000—to Rome, unlike some of his brother-monarchs, who kept half for themselves. Henry additionally integrated the rule of Church and State by appointing only ecclesiastics as his chancellors, and the control of clerical appointments was arranged to the satisfaction of both sides. Chapters were always willing to elect and the Papacy to provide the king's nominees, who were foreigners only when he chose. The Papacy on its part aided Henry in maintaining ordered civil government, by, for example, regulating the rights of sanctuary and, by a statesmanlike Bull confirmed by Alexander VI, ordering traitors in sanctuary to be guarded by royal officers. When there was a clash of the royal and papal authorities—as throughout history everywhere in Europe there inevitably was at times—it was amicably settled, and the earlier statutes of Provisors and Praemunire, passed over a century before, were kept well in the background. The purpose of

---

[1] Non-Catholic readers unfamiliar with the actual time-sequence may find the following epitome of interest. By 1540 the last of the religious houses had been destroyed: in 1541 Henry started to prepare his Primer (the precursor of the Prayer Book) which was issued in 1545, superseding Hindsley's Primer published in 1539. In November 1547 the Chantries Act authorized new spoliations: in April 1548 the Protector Somerset sold (in modern currency) £150,000 worth of his share of them, which sum, according to Professor Pollard, was "an infinitesimal part of the whole" amount realized by the confiscations; in September 1548 Cranmer and the bishops started to discuss the preparation of the new Prayer Book embodying the new doctrines. It was only an interim measure, as Cranmer explained to a meeting of foreign Protestants in the April of 1549, "lest excessive changes should repel the people." It was completed and imposed on the country by an Act of Uniformity in January 1549. After the popular rebellion it provoked had been crushed, an Order, dated 4 November 1550, was issued for the destruction of all altars, accompanied by letters to bishops giving arguments they should use to reconcile their parishioners to the loss of the ornaments of their churches. In the Convocation of December 1550 and in meetings between Cranmer and the bishops during the January of 1551, plans, were made for the final version of the Prayer Book, which was completed and enforced, by a second Act of Uniformity, in the April of 1552. This marks the moment when, officially, England became Protestant in doctrine—twenty-one years after the beginning of the Reformation and when the economic and political revolution had been carried through to the end.

Provisors was to defeat the Pope's claim to provide the personnel of all English bishoprics, and of Praemunire, to protect the temporal jurisdiction of the king against any wrongful infringement by the Pope. They had been brought into being at the time when the Church was rent by the Babylonish Captivity and the Great Schism. The effect of them then was to make Pope Martin V comment bitterly: "It is not the Pope but the King of England who governs the Church in his dominions;" but their purpose was to safeguard the good government of the Church in England in a time of unpredictable chaos abroad.

In the reign of Henry VII and the early years of his son, it had been demonstrated that national interests were compatible with papal supremacy without any recourse to such legalism; but the limits of the royal power had been also explicitly defined and it was agreed on all sides that "no temporal act can make a temporal man have spiritual jurisdiction"—that the king, for example, could not, of himself, interfere with tithes since "a temporal act without the assent of the Supreme Head [that is, the Pope] cannot make the King a Parson".

This state of affairs, in which Henry VIII until he wished to "get a divorce" (to use the popular phraseology) enthusiastically concurred, worked admirably. But when the king, for his own reasons, wished to overthrow it, the majority of people might be forgiven if they saw, in its initial stages, nothing more than the reopening of an old political debate, which did not affect the Faith.

But from the vantage point of posterity we see that what is called the Reformation in England was accomplished within the span of a lifetime of seventy-five years and that the first definite act of it was in 1531 when the English bishops acknowledged King Henry VIII as Supreme Head of the Church in England "as far as the law of Christ allows"—a saving clause which made the innovation look hardly more than a debating-motion. But the end of it was the penal anti-Catholic legislation of 1606 which made the reception of Anglican Holy Communion the prerequisite of holding office in the State, and which imposed an Oath of Allegiance so framed that no Catholic could possibly take it. And what, religiously speaking, had been accomplished by the Reformers in that short space of seventy-five years left no doubt in anyone's mind as to the nature of what, in fact, had happened.

By 1606, throughout the length and breadth of England, no monastery or nunnery or shrine or chantry existed; to say Mass or to attend Mass, to make a convert to Catholicism or to be a convert were all punishable by death; an Oath asserting that the Head of the Church in England was the successor of Henry VIII instead of the successor of St. Peter was obligatory on all persons of whatever rank under the penalty of exclusion from places of trust and from all the liberal professions; Catholics were required not only to attend Protestant churches but to take Communion there under pain of the confiscation of two-thirds of their property; they were debarred from the legal and medical professions, from the army and the universities and, if they sent their children abroad to be educated as Catholics, their inheritance was taken away from them and given to their Protestant relations, who were encouraged by liberal bribes to inform against them. In England there was no crucifix to be seen or any statue of Christ's Mother in any public place and that none should remain as private relics in Catholic homes, Justices of the Peace were given indiscriminate right of search; if any crucifix were there discovered the figure was to be publicly defaced at the Quarter Sessions.

This is but a part of the transformation, which was enforced by that army of spies, *agents provocateurs*, forgers and torturers that forms so prominent a feature of Elizabethan England. The mainspring of the movement, moreover, was still, at the end as at the beginning, property. The religious theory continued to safeguard the secular practice. To return to the Faith might have meant to have to return the loot. An abbey might have become an abbey once more instead of the favourite residence of a Protestant landowner. And it was this secular avarice allied with this secret fear which made and kept England Protestant—a fear that continued till the eve of the eighteenth century when the last counterattack made by the last Catholic king (a convert to the Faith) was defeated by foreign invasion and the Crown itself was added to the spoils.

To understand how the mass of the nation was coerced into accepting the change—for the common people were the victims rather than the beneficiaries of the economic revolution—it is probably easiest to look at the analogy of Soviet Russia in our own century. An effective power to enforce obedience and "make examples" of the disobedient; an effective propaganda, unwearying and unceasing, to falsify the past and "explain" the present; a coherent ideology for the satisfaction of intellectuals; a patriotism engendered by representing all diplomatic or military nationalist movements as defensive actions against powerful ideological aggressors; and, above all, an "Iron Curtain" to prevent the dissemination of the truth from outside civilizations—these as effectively

prevent a Russian born to-day from understanding the realities of Russia in 1917 as they prevented an Englishman born in 1571 from knowing what happened in 1531.

Yet though the methods of a police state may be to a certain extent effective internally, whatever the relationship of the revolutionary country to the world outside, it is an enforced isolation which is the most important factor in ensuring success. The Act of State in England had, at the very beginning, to provide a safeguard against outside interference, since it was challenging the basic assumption of contemporary Western civilization—that there was a spiritual Head above and apart from national secular interests. The first step in—to use the later terminology—"lowering the Iron Curtain" was the "Act in Restraint of Appeals" which deprived Englishmen of their right to appeal to the international, and internationally recognized, jurisdiction of Rome.

This Act, passed in 1533, is crucial. One Protestant historian has described it as constitutionally "the most important of the sixteenth century if not of any century" and another, in a justly famous passage, has written that its Preamble is "remarkable partly because it manufactured history on an unprecedented scale, but chiefly because it has operated from that day to this as a powerful incentive to the manufacture by others upon some similar lines."

By officially inventing past history, it laid the foundations of the basic myth, still monotonously repeated in textbooks, of a sturdy Imperial race defying a "foreign" Pope; but its short-term effect, immediate and practical, was to cut England off from Christendom. It enforced insularity and when the generation born in the year of its passing were in their maturity England was no longer "Mary's Dowry" and an integral part of Europe, but the isolated island of Queen Elizabeth, with a new and strange system of belief and worship and a novel pattern of tyranny.

This isolation in its turn dictated the "missionary activity" which is so difficult for non-Catholics to appreciate at its true value. The succession of heroic men who "trod the Via Dolorosa from Douai to Tyburn" were inflamed only by love of souls. The missions were in no sense political, as the Government propaganda machine necessarily insisted that they were. They were as nakedly religious as the missions a millennium earlier.

Just as once the Saxons, in destroying the Roman civilization, had so obliterated the Catholic Church in Britain that the Pope had to send Augustine to preach the Faith anew to a pagan *ultima Thule*, so now, a thousand years later, Rome had once again to send her missionary priests to face martyrdom in a lapsed and lost land. The superficial differences between the sixth and sixteenth centuries are obvious enough, yet the sixty years between the defeat and death of King Arthur at Camlan in 537 and St. Augustine's exposition of Christianity before King Ethelbert's court in 597 are not in spirit remote from the interim between the passing of the Act of Appeals in 1533 and Blessed Edmund Campion's defence in 1581 before Queen Elizabeth's court of the religion which Augustine had taught. And as Augustine could have pointed back across the change and the chaos to St. Alban, who had died for Christ in Verulamium, so Campion, about to die for Christ in London, could invoke "all the ancient priests, bishops and kings—all that was once the glory of England, the Island of Saints and the most devoted child of the See of Peter" to bear witness against their "degenerate descendants."

Of the Roman Catholic theologians speaking from a European background, Father GEORGES TAVARD (b. 1922) is perhaps one of the best known today. A member of the order of the Augustinians of the Assumption, he taught theology in a Roman Catholic college in Surrey, England, for three years and then became chairman of the department of theology at Mount Mercy College, Pittsburgh. He is greatly interested in the whole question of Roman Catholic–Protestant relations, particularly in the possibility of the reunion of the two bodies. Because of his writings, he was a Roman Catholic observer at the Conference on Faith and Order of the World Council of Churches at Montreal in 1963. In 1962, he was a theological expert for Vatican Council II.*

▶ ## *Similarity Between Reformation Doctrines and Catholic Beliefs*

The essential inspiration of the Reformation is to be found in the insistence of the reformers on the doctrine of justification. Christianity is a doctrine of salvation, of deliverance; it assumes a state of bondage of which everyone has an experience, saying with St Paul: "My own actions bewilder me; what I do is not what I wish to do, but something which I hate." Slaves of sin and the devil, men are set free by a unique mediator, Jesus Christ: without the Saviour, there is neither salvation nor deliverance. "Grace" is the gift of that deliverance, the divine act by which the holiness with which Christ is holy overflows on to sin-

ners. Thus are we made holy and justified and this justification is a pure gift. "Faith" is the human response to Christ, the acceptance of a righteousness which cannot come from ourselves and which we do not merit. It carries with it love for him who has given it to us, and the hope (that is, supernatural certitude) that God does not repent of his gifts; again according to St Paul: ". . . so called, he justified them; so justified, he glorified them."

Luther was fond of setting the "law" against the "good news." The Law, laid down by the Old Testament, looked for fear and obedience; by its strict enact-

* From the book *Protestantism* by Georges Tavard. Copyright © 1959 by Hawthorne Books, Inc. Published by Hawthorne Books, Inc., 70 Fifth Avenue, New York, New York. Chapter 11. Most footnotes omitted.

ments, man was condemned and his essentially sinful state was revealed. The Good News announced by the Saviour was that, henceforth, the Law was abolished: there was now only Christian liberty. This liberty comes from divine justification, from grace, and sinful man has the assurance of it in his conscience through faith.

There is no contradiction here of Catholic theology, but it must be remembered that, in Luther's thought as in Calvin's, Catholic theology was something quite different from the traditional expression of the message of the Gospel. At the heart of the Church's teaching and practice the reformers certainly recognized the Gospel; but they held that this, the Christian soul of the Church, was buried deep and stifled under a mass of human inventions.

Of course they knew that they were not the first to teach the free pardon of sins. St Paul and St Augustine, whom they explicitly invoked, had clearly affirmed it; St Thomas Aquinas had taken it as the principle of a majestic theology of grace. The commentaries on St Paul by the great humanists of the end of the fifteenth century, notably that of James Lefèbvre d'Étaples (1456–1537), set forth the Pauline interpretation of free justification by faith; and the saints of the Church, especially the Rhenish mystics of the fourteenth and fifteenth centuries, Eckhart, Tauler and Suso, described the absolute dominion of the living God over the passive soul. Luther, who was not very familiar with true Thomism, had been influenced by the mystics and the humanists. But neither he nor Calvin would allow that this line of thought deriving from the Gospel was in agreement with the teaching of the

Roman Church. The most widely held theological opinion, that of the nominalist Gabriel Biel (1425–1495), inclined towards a freedom of the will which was closely related to the old heresy of Pelagianism—man could earn his salvation through the efforts of his own asceticism. There is some danger here of our Saviour's rôle being transformed: instead of saving, he gives an example. What, then, becomes of the new creature, the new man that, according to the Gospel, the Christian is? What becomes of the new creation inaugurated by baptism? A whole aspect of Catholic tradition is obscured.

When Luther was condemned, he drew the conclusion that the Roman Church denied the central thesis of his remonstrance of 1517, that the true treasure-house of the Church is the most holy Good News of the glory and the grace of God, and so the Roman Church gradually assumed in his eyes certain aspects of antichrist. When Calvin contemplated its piety, he saw, along with the traffic in indulgences and Masses, the exploitation of doubtful relics: "It is a notorious fact that most of the relics which are shown everywhere are false, and have been produced by scoffers, who have impudently imposed on the unhappy world."

Now, according to the traditional maxim, *lex orandi, lex credendi*, that is, practice expresses the belief; Protestantism undertook the task of purifying both practice and beliefs through a return to the original purity of the Gospel.

Concern about purifying faith was not confined to Protestants. Spirituality of the most traditional kind shows clearly that faith is not always pure; a vast human element mingles with it in the mind of the Christian, where flesh wars with the spirit. Nor is the unfathomable nature of the divinity diminished in the Incarnation: the God who reveals himself in Jesus Christ remains the unknowable God. To purify faith means precisely to commit oneself to God, unknowable in himself, but known, although only partially, in Jesus Christ. This demands a complete renunciation of all that is not him, of human forms of expression in their inadequacy and of the human desire to reduce God to our own image and likeness. Idolatry does not consist only in adoring creatures; there is also a more subtle idolatry, the substitution of pious imaginings or theological speculation for the revelation of the Bible. To do this is to replace the glory of God by human pride.

The Protestant desire to purify faith is derived from these sound principles of Catholic spirituality, but because of a false start a field was opened in which their application became extremely delicate. Of course, individual Christians often fall into spiritual idolatry; the struggle between the flesh and the spirit must entail occasional defeats, and the purification of faith is an elementary duty of the Christian life. But Luther did not confine himself to that. Not satisfied with purifying his own faith and that of his disciples, he wished to purge the faith of the Church itself. To take the faith of the Church and examine the body of its teaching, to subject dogmatic decrees to searching examination, to doubt the decisions of supreme authority, amounted to transposing the problem into a realm which until then had always been held illegitimate by universal tradition. At this point, the Church of Rome, entrusted with the deposit of revelation, met the reformers with an absolute negative.

This opposition of the Church came as no surprise to Protestant reasoning, which saw it as one aspect of the idolatry which had gradually crept into the teaching of the magisterium itself. It confirmed Luther's assertion that the human authorities of the Church claimed divine authority; human words paraded under the guise of the Word of God itself. As always, the subjective faith of each believer must be purified, but it was also necessary in his view to sift the objective faith of the Church as a whole.

Following Luther, the Protestant religion desires therefore that every age should reexamine the data of faith bequeathed to it by the preceding one; ecclesiastical tradition must be constantly verified by recourse to the Scriptures. Having denied the infallibility of the hierarchy, Luther reduced Christianity in principle to the explicit teachings of the Scriptures; no longer was there room for the development of dogma or progressive unfolding of the primitive deposit of faith. Calvin's theological undertaking in writing *The Institutes* was an experimental confrontation of this purity and simplicity of Scripture with the speculative powers of the Christian spirit.

The works of the Reformation must be read with this in mind. Whether it is the work of Calvin himself, the most impressive of them all, Zwingli's *Commentarius de Vera et Falsa Religione*, Melanchthon's *Loci Communes* or Bucer's *De Regno Dei, The Decades* of Bullinger or the productions of smaller scope by their emulators, all aspire to be nothing more than a faithful echo of the teachings of the Gospel. The numerous Confessions of Faith themselves were intended to be no more. The seventeenth century saw the proliferation of theological schools and the development of what we call Protestant orthodoxy. This was the age of vast theological works, both Lutheran and Calvinist, which imitated the Catholic theological Summas; a great part of the scholastic system and method diffused itself in Protestant thought and yet not one of these theologians claimed to propound a synthesis that was not strictly in the purest spirit of return to Gospel sources.

From where, then, did Luther obtain his idea of reform? Protestantism is founded on a kind of generalized mysticism in which the mystical requirement of a radical purification of faith is unduly extended to the institution of the Church herself. But none of the great Christian mystics had demanded the renunciation of tradition in favour of Scripture alone; neither St Bernard (1090–1153), nor Richard of St Victor (1104–1173), nor the mystics of the Rhineland set up Scripture against the Church. Luther's source, if he had one on this point, was certainly not to be found in orthodox mystical tradition.

As for the theological tradition, Protestants claimed the patronage of the Englishman, John Wyclif (*c.* 1324–1384) and of the Czech, John Huss (*c.* 1369–1415), who were both heterodox theologians, the latter having been condemned to the stake by the Council of Constance. But neither of them strayed from the traditional concept of Scripture. Medieval theology in general, St Thomas's as well as St Bonaventure's or Duns Scotus', had not elaborated an explicit doctrine of the sources of faith. It is enough to read the beginning of the *Summa Theologica* to see that Thomist reasoning knows only the "sacred teaching" as the source of faith. But the Middle Ages read and understood Scripture through the practice and faith of

the Church: the Church was the infallible interpreter of the divine Word. On this, the teaching of the great doctors, although unsystematic, was unswerving.

Luther did not know the great scholastics well. In fact, the divorce of Scripture from the Church is to be discerned in the thought of some lesser theologians. At the end of the thirteenth century Henry of Ghent (1213–1293) put forward the possibility of an opposition between Scripture and a church which was the Church only in the eyes of men and not in reality; in the fourteenth century, Gregory of Rimini (†1358) declared that the Church was not "a principle of theological thought," as all theological thought took its rise from the Canon of Scripture alone. Gregory, himself also an Augustinian friar, was, indeed, one of the principal sources of Luther's thought. Nearer his own times, certain of the humanists of the Low Countries had extended to faith what Gregory had stated about theological thought. So in formulating his principle of Scripture only, Luther was able to point to predecessors. But neither Henry of Ghent nor Gregory of Rimini had invoked Scripture against the Church. But Luther did so.

To speak of invoking Scripture against the Church is not the exact Protestant terminology: the reformers did not want to condemn the Church, but to save it. Calvin says: "If the Christian Church was at all times founded on the preaching of the apostles and the books of the prophets, then the sanction for such a doctrine must precede the Church, which indeed it helps to form, as the foundation comes before the building." To do the opposite, to raise the building before the foundations by emancipating the Church from Scripture, is "to create an over-riding tyranny under the great name of the Church." The Church may be recognized by her fidelity to Scripture, and to ensure that fidelity is to do a service to the Church.

If Scripture is the only source of faith and the sole foundation of the Church, it is because it is not just a collection of doctrines but God's mouthpiece in a unique manner. Luther himself was very free, too free with it, in fact; he ranked the books according to their greater or lesser agreement with the doctrine of justification. This was rather like turning Scripture against itself, but it was chiefly a way, if a too facile one, of insisting on the importance of justification and grace. Calvin, more logically and less paradoxically, did not thus venture into passing judgement on the Word of God.

Both of them, and classical Protestantism with them, heard in Scripture the living Word of God. For Luther, justification by faith was the act of divine condescension coming to man through the Incarnation; Scripture, in bringing this message, does not become a second principle side by side with this first one, on the contrary, it is the form which free justification takes, the Good News. Justification and Scripture are two parts of one whole; in scholastic terms, they are "matter" and "form," the one unable to exist without the other.

Equally for Calvin, Scripture is a living word, the Spirit which bears scriptural witness within us. Christians cannot, then, read it as mere words, it is spirit and life, and if we are to know it as the Word of God, the Spirit must bear witness in our hearts as we read: "It is necessary that the same Spirit who spoke by the mouth of the prophets should enter our hearts, and pierce them to the depths, that they may be convinced that the prophets have faithfully announced what was commanded them from on high." The witness of the Spirit is an inward illumination; but this does not permit anyone to evolve an eccentric form of Christianity according to his own private judgement, for he who reads Scripture in the light of the Spirit has no private judgement: "Above all human judgement, we conclude without doubt that Scripture has been given to us out of the mouth of God himself, through the ministry of men, as if we saw God therein with our own eyes." This is not reserved for a small élite: "I say quite clearly that each of the faithful should make trial for himself." To know the truth of Scripture is faith's daily experience.

From the Catholic point of view, this is not a false approach. In so far as it sets aside the infallible Church, Protestant theology is incomplete; but its solicitude that nothing should be false to the Word of God is inherited from uninterrupted Catholic tradition. The trouble was that, in the sixteenth century, tradition touching this point was in partial eclipse. The Council of Trent formulated it afresh in 1546, but in terms that the reformed churches, after a generation of Protestantism, could no longer understand.

The whole of Protestantism in its origins is expressed by this bracketing of justification and Scripture: the principle of the absolute sovereignty of God is represented subjectively by free justification and objectively by Scripture. Calvin's doctrine of predestination to heaven or hell is a conclusion drawn from this. Very fortunately, the mass of Protestants have not followed his inflexible reasoning on this point; there is a logic of love which refuses to accept the rational logic of Calvinist predestination. In fact, the twofold predestination envisaged by Calvin, which he himself called "the horrible decree," is anthropomorphic in conception; it implies that the divine thought and will moves in a human manner. But the two qualities that man finds it most difficult to reconcile are in perfect harmony with God, so that he wills at the same time the punishment of the sinner and his salvation; it is always justice and love, not justice for some and love for others, as Calvin saw it. By the end of the sixteenth century the doctrine of predestination was under attack by many Protestants themselves.

There are other doctrines frequently attributed to the reformers which justifiably give rise to misgiving. In his book, *The Spirit & Forms of Protestantism*, Fr Louis Bouyer has shown that the reformers implicitly contradicted themselves. On the one hand, the principles of the Reformation were eminently Catholic in their positive aspect; on the other, Luther and Calvin's theological systematization introduced new elements which nullified these principles. Thus it was with the concept of "extrinsic" justification: according to this, the justice with which Christ makes us just[1] is only "imputed" to us, it does not sanctify us

[1] The Latin, *justitia*, and the Greek, *dikaiosune*, are usually rendered in English as justice or righteousness, with the adjectives, just and righteous. These have both acquired somewhat misleading juridical or moral connotation; the concept, as may be seen by the context here, is something closer to holiness in its fullest sense. (*Trans.*)

within. These terms are found in Protestant writings, but in using them, the intention of the reformers must be remembered.

If we take the words literally, a purely extrinsic justification cannot make us just in anybody's eyes. The *fiat* which saves us must be a creative *fiat*: it causes what it enunciates, and it makes us just in complete reality. Is this denied by the reformers? It would appear not. When they asserted imputed justification, they wished simply to deny a justice pertaining to man; they wished to make Pelagian distortions of sanctification impossible, to kill at the roots the "idolatrous" desire to sanctify oneself through an accumulation of merits. In other words, imputed justification has a very profound sense if we truly understand the thought of the reformers; the inmost being of the Christian is no longer the sinful creature that it was before Christ, but a being-in-Christ, and it is in Christ's own Person that we receive forgiveness, salvation and grace, sanctification and glory. We have nothing of our own: all comes from Christ. As men we are sinners, but as Christians we are saved. Thus, as the Lutheran saying puts it, the Christian is "always sinful, always penitent, always justified"; sinful in himself, his justification is Christ: "God acquits us of guilt by extending to us the justice which pertains to the Lord Jesus." There is no doubt that this is the sense of the term "imputation." Calvin makes it explicit: "From this it follows clearly that we are justified in the sight of God by means of the justice of Christ alone; that is, man is not just in himself but only through the justice of Christ which he receives through imputation." So "imputed" justice is given to man in a real way. The ambiguity of the term "imputation" is regrettable, but once this has been cleared up, the doctrine is not so objectionable.

The reformers were more interested in the redeeming action of Christ than in the effect of that action in the transformation of the Christian soul. Perhaps this is why Protestantism quickly worked out a complementary concept, the inward assurance of justification. Free justification cannot be determined by its fruits, because this would tend to encourage once again superstitious ideas about personal merits. How then are we to know for certain that we are Christians? Here it must be remembered that, to the Lutheran, faith is not just an assent but that it implies also confidence in the merits of Christ. But anyone who has confidence must be aware that he has it, and here is the assurance of faith as envisaged by Luther and Calvin.

In spite of some of the more extreme formulas, it would seem that this assurance was not originally considered to be an integral part of faith; far from denying faith to those who did not yet enjoy the fullness of Christian liberty, Calvin wished "to help timid consciences make their peace with God, whether these consciences labour in doubts over the remission of their sins, or are in fear and solicitude as to whether their works, imperfect and defiled with the stains of the flesh, are pleasing to God." Christian liberty, freed from fears and doubts, and a "handmaid of justification," comes from trust in Jesus Christ alone; it is a fruit of faith, not faith itself. Faith is "a firm and certain knowledge of God's good will towards us; this knowledge is founded on the free promise given by Jesus Christ and is revealed to our understanding and confirmed in our hearts by the Holy Spirit."

This thing revealed to our understanding and confirmed in our hearts cannot be illusory; faith, true to itself, is not the sentiment of a slave, but of a son, so it cannot feel any doubt about the efficacy of salvation. As it develops normally, faith carries along with itself the assurance of justification. Protestant terminology lends itself to misunderstanding, but fundamentally it includes in its analysis of faith what Catholic theologians usually attribute to the virtue of hope.

Thus the Council of Trent condemned a slightly different position; it cannot be maintained that "man, born again and justified, must believe as of faith that he is one of the number of the predestined." It is easy to see how their disciples and their adversaries misinterpreted the thought of the reformers as implying a doctrine of justification by assurance, an assurance of one's own predestination. Once again, the formulas that were employed were very unfortunate.

Free justification, Scripture and faith are the essence of Protestant doctrine; when properly understood there is no irreducible fundamental contradiction between them and Catholic doctrine. Terms like imputed justification and assurance were ill-chosen and lent themselves too easily to mistakes in interpretation. Once past the early years of the Reformation, the consequence is seen in this characteristic error, the transition to justification by assurance.

To avoid equal misconceptions, Catholics must complete the reformers' explanations, correcting their viewpoint and, still more, seeking correspondence of thought beneath the divergences of language. They must take particular care not to confuse the doctrine of the reformers with certain of its subsequent deformations. If these precautions are adopted, it will then be seen how much closer is the profound spirituality of the Protestant mind to Catholicism than it believes itself to be.

As a Roman Catholic layman, PIERRE JANELLE (b. 1891), for many years a professor at the Université de Clermont, came to the study of the Reformation with a somewhat different perspective from that of his coreligionists. The title of the book from which this selection is taken, *The Catholic Reformation*, indicates that he does not regard the sixteenth-century movement of reform within the Roman Catholic Church as primarily a counterattack against Protestantism. Rather, he sees it as a true and very necessary movement of reform which remained orthodox while the Protestant movement, responding to the same stimuli, became heretical.*

Anarchy: The Disease Within the Church

In one of the scenes of Marlow's *Doctor Faustus*—here a mere reproduction of its German source—we are introduced into the pope's private chamber at the Vatican. Mephistopheles asks Faustus, who is eager to go and admire the marvels of ancient Rome, to stay awhile:

I know you'd fain see the Pope,
And take some part of holy Peter's feast,
Where thou shalt see a troop of bald-pate friars,
Whose *summum bonum* is in belly-cheer.

Then the pope and the "Cardinal of Lorrain . . . enter to the banquet, with friars attending." They sit down at table, while the friars bring in "dainty dishes" sent by the bishop of Milan and the car-

dinal of Florence. But Faustus, who is invisible, snatches the food from them, and is therefore cursed "with bell, book, and candle." The scene is, of course, a farce, and an unduly coarse one; yet it can hardly be termed a pure libel. That the moral condition of the clergy, and especially of the Roman Curia, had by the end of the fifteenth century become deplorable, is asserted by eminent Catholic writers of the time, whose evidence cannot be gainsaid. The spirit of lucre and sensuousness was manifested in many abuses, especially various forms of simony, which were in urgent need of reformation.

There was no need, however, of reformation such as the Protestants under-

* Reprinted from P. Janelle, *The Catholic Reformation* (Milwaukee, Wis.: The Bruce Publishing Company, 1963), Chap. I.

stood it. According to their contention, the primitive simplicity of the Church had become disfigured by manifold superstitions, these being in turn the source of the lowering of her morality. Remove these superstitions, purge Christian doctrine of an excessive belief in the supernatural and marvelous, relieve Christian discipline of the strain of excessive asceticism, and order would be restored.

Now, if such a view were true, if medieval superstition had engendered corruption, the "Eve of the Reformation" ought to appear as a particularly barren period, both in regard to devotion and virtue. A careful study of the late fifteenth and early sixteenth centuries, however, shows that there was, at the time, a flowering forth of piety and mysticism. The question then arises, how could the above-mentioned abuses be met with in the midst of so much faith and charity? This strange contradiction is to be accounted for, not by false beliefs, but by defective organization, and consequently defective discipline.

The Church had become cut up into a number of independently functioning bodies; authority, jurisdiction, and possessions were divided among them, and inextricably entangled. This, on the one hand, made the enforcement of ecclesiastical canons and regulations extremely difficult, and provided numberless loopholes whereby to evade them. On the other hand, the struggle of many conflicting interests gave rise to constant litigation. It heightened, at the expense of the regular hierarchy, the importance of those officials who were empowered to settle differences and who were too often tempted to take bribes or to exact undue payments. This was especially the case when favors were sought from the Roman Curia. There was an understanding between those who sued for dispensations or exemptions from the performance of their clerical duties or the observance of disciplinary rules, and those who granted graces against payment for the benefit of the papal exchequer or to fill their own pockets. Money assumed as much importance in the Church as in any temporal state, and where money reigns supreme, sloth, lechery, pride inevitably follow.

Thus the moral disorders in the Church really had their source in the overgrown development of an officialdom, the members of which had come to identify the Church with their own class. Reformation had to hack pitilessly through a network of vested interests; it could come only from the authority that had connived at the abuses, and must now, in correcting them, correct itself. The result would be a strong papacy, supported by a strong and independent hierarchy, which would be less likely to let its own dignity and prestige be debased in the eyes of Christendom.

Unfortunately centrifugal tendencies had been at work since the time of the Great Schism, and the Councils of Basle and Constance. These two councils had met as a response to the general clamor for reform; but in fact they ushered in the spirit of nationalism, which was to be the main obstacle in the way of reform. The various European sovereigns cared little for the moral welfare of the Church; they preferred to consider her as a department of the State, to take her dignitaries into their employment, and use her preferments and benefices as rewards for their loyal subjects; thus countenancing abuses which they were later to denounce, once they had found it to their advantage to chastise the Church by seizing her property. Even when they were not actively hostile to the work of reformation from inside, they refused to give up their private quarrels and claims in order to ensure general peace; and the correction of abuses in a divided Europe remained well-nigh impossible.

In fact, whatever may be said about the corruption of the Holy See, it was not altogether the fault of the popes if they had little time to attend to such matters as monastic discipline or the education of the lower clergy. Whether they liked it or not, their safety, their independence, nay, all but the very existence of the papacy, were involved in the wars between the European princes. They were threatened by the French or Imperial invasions of Italy, or by the Turkish advance. They had to struggle painfully to defend their temporal dominions, which alone could ensure their spiritual independence and authority. Had they not contrived to hold their own against national interests, there might never have been a Catholic Reformation at all.

They might, it is true, have taken less account of political dangers and inconveniences, and attempted to carry Christian opinion along with them, by boldly asserting their will to perform the task of reformation under any circumstances. But they had become too much absorbed in worldly matters to realize the driving force of a purely spiritual appeal. The Renaissance had not merely corrupted the personal morality of the popes and their court; it had done even worse in lowering their notion of their proper function. For apostleship, it had substituted "policy," the art of playing upon human passions and motives.

Taken as a whole, the condition of the Curia was such as to make any Christian blush. Its bureaucracy was self-centered and self-seeking; it had come to halo its privileges, its greed, and its lusts with the sacred character of Christianity itself. Only a huge evangelical revival could breed enough of the spirit of sacrifice in the Church, to sweep away all selfishness; and in fact the Catholic Reformation was due first and foremost to a reawakening of the spirit of the Gospel. But it would still have failed to achieve success if it had merely been a reversion to the intellectual and sentimental outlook of the Middle Ages. It would not have been possible to fall back upon the Renaissance; it must perforce be made use of toward a Christian end.

Such was the task of the movement known as "Christian humanism," which began about 1470 and was steadily gathering strength in the early sixteenth century. It served a double purpose: it saved the Church from paganism, while retaining, in the philosophy, literature, and art of the ancients, whatever might serve toward enriching Christian life. Hence its peculiar quality, which was new and attractive, and which St. Thomas More represents better than anyone else. It was fully flourishing before Luther arose, and was likely to blossom into further flowers of wisdom and holiness, when the religious war forced it for a time into the background. Yet it was to come to the front again with the Council of Trent and the Society of Jesus, and henceforth to be one of the chief elements of the Catholic Reformation.

According to early Protestant controversialists, such as Tyndale, the abuses in the Church were the consequence of false doctrine. A close study of fifteenth-century conditions brings us, however, to a wholly different conclusion. The abuses may be shown to have sprung, not from mistaken notions on justification, the worship of the saints, Purgatory, etc., but from the state of administrative anarchy which had prevailed since the Great Schism. In the early centuries, the organization of the Church, aside from the divinely instituted headship of Peter and his successors, had been modeled on that of the Roman Empire: there was a regular hierarchy, gradually descending from the pope of Rome to the primates, metropolitans, bishops, and deacons. With the advent of feudalism however, this fine architectural order had been in many ways disturbed. As in civil society, many smaller, self-governing units had been founded, which did not come under the authority of the ordinary superiors. There was not much harm in this, so long as the Holy See was strong enough to assert its general overlordship. But when it had become enfeebled by the Great Schism and the conciliar movement, it was unable to put a stop to the scrimmage which took place between all sorts of ecclesiastical bodies. The authority of the hierarchy was openly flouted by clerical or lay patrons, cathedral chapters, religious orders and houses; this being made easier by the practice of exemption, which national sovereigns naturally enough turned into a weapon against Church independence, but which the popes, in a misguided attempt to extend their jurisdiction, were themselves imprudent enough to foster.

Whatever efforts the bishops might make toward a general reformation of morals were set at naught from the fact that they were unable to compel the obedience of a very large section of their clergy. In the late fifteenth century, many parishes were really in the hands of clerical patrons, generally religious houses, which held the advowsons and drew the tithes, often from a consider-

able distance. Such patrons were obviously unable to help in the enforcement of Church discipline, and were mainly intent on the maintenance of their rights. In the diocese of Paris, for instance, out of 469 parishes, the bishop appointed only 215 incumbents. In Paris itself, the episcopal appointments were only 6 out of 30; worst of all, in the diocese of Lyons, only 21 parishes out of 392 were in the hands of the archbishop.

Nor was the disciplinary influence of the bishops merely countervailed by the power of the patrons. The various religious communities that had come into being inside each diocese also asserted their independence. Cathedral chapters, collegiate churches, brotherhoods of secular priests, monasteries, priories, or convents, all had their elected heads, their assemblies, their statutes, and their estates; they had vassals and tenants, and commanded considerable influence. Besides, most of the chapters, many collegiate churches, all the greater monasteries, and such religious orders as the Carthusians and mendicant friars, had been granted by the Holy See exemption from episcopal jurisdiction. Within their boundaries, they exercised sovereign powers and through the incumbents of their benefices, they held whole blocks of parishes under their sway. The authority of the bishops was threatened with total disappearance.

The practice of exemption was steadily growing in the fifteenth century, and it is but natural that the bishops should have attempted to minimize its effects. Hence a permanent struggle, which led in many cases to scandalous disorders. At Vendôme, the bishop, having entered the collegiate church by stealth, was surrounded by the monks, insulted, and mishandled; the abbot tore from him his rochet, his square cap, and "part of the hair of his head"; then he was seized by the hands and feet, and flung into the street, amidst the shouting of the mob. Similar happenings occurred, between 1470 and 1515, in a great many places in France. Cathedral chapters were equally unruly. They were composed of men of learning, and had great social influence, besides their actual share in the government of cathedral towns, and their powers over a numerous retinue. The late fifteenth century is a period of constant wrangling between chapters and bishops. Both parties go to law over the most trifling points—precedence in a procession, or the whipping of a choirboy. In 1517, the canons of Langres manifest their displeasure to the archbishop by regularly standing up and having the bells rung when they reach the following verse of Lauds: *"Fiant dies ejus pauci et episcopatum ejus recipiat alter."* Even the archdeacons try to extend their authority at the expense of the bishops. What wonder, then, that the latter should have turned in disgust from their religious duties, in which they found rebellion on every hand, to the field of political life, and willingly accepted the favor which princes offered to them in exchange for their able service?

They did try, however, to countercheck the encroachments of exempt bodies; but the means they used still further increased the disorder in the Church. Just as the popes peopled the Curia and the College of Cardinals with their own kin, because other appointments would have been unsafe, the bishops endeavored to open the cathedral chapters to their relatives, thus laying themselves open to the charge of nepotism. In regard to the religious houses, since they could not be held in curb, the simplest plan was to gain a footing inside them. Therefore, in the latter half of the fifteenth century, monastic dignities were more and more frequently conferred upon members of the hierarchy. The circumstances were in favor of such a change, for both the popes and kings wished to have the greatest possible number of benefices in their gift and discountenanced the old practice of appointing abbots, priors, and other officers by election. Thus in France the episcopate easily acquired control over the largest and richest abbeys, such as Saint-Denis, Fécamp, or La Chaise-Dieu, and even over most of the houses of the Cistercian Order. Obviously the prelates, who held abbacies *in commendam*, could not fulfill the duties of their change. Hence, the monasteries were ruled by deputies, from whom the flaming enthusiasm of the founders or reformers of religious orders could certainly not be expected.

But, it will be asked, was the increase of monastic influence in the fifteen century necessarily an evil? About the answer there can be little doubt. In the early Middle Ages, indeed, the religious orders had spread culture and true religion everywhere, and the work they had then done toward civilizing Europe can scarcely be overestimated. But conditions had changed, and the old spirit of heroic enterprise had been largely superseded by remissness and perfunctoriness. To such decay there were, of course, exceptions, which will be mentioned in due course. In Northern Europe especially, in the Low Countries, Germany, and England, the monastic spirit had not exhausted its powers of recuperation and creation. Yet, it cannot be doubted that, as a whole, conditions in most monasteries left much to be desired. Here again, a process of administrative disorganization, far more than any "superstitions," was at the root of moral evils. Discipline could be enforced only by a central authority, which in the religious orders was that of the general chapter, held at regular intervals, and strong enough to compel obedience. Now in the fifteenth century, the general tendency is toward disintegration. The various houses of each order tended to loosen the bonds which united them to the others, and to assert their independence.

This was, of course, easily achieved in the case of the so-called "autocephalous" monasteries, which had been the earliest-founded, and mostly belonged to the Benedictine Order. The drawbacks attending their isolation had become apparent in the fourteenth century, and Pope Benedict XII, through his bull *Summi Magistri*, had attempted to gather those of France into six provinces. The system, however, soon broke down, and many large monasteries, living for and by themselves, came to assume the position of great landowners rather than of religious institutions. But the same individualism was equally at work in those monastic orders which up till then had constituted real federations, with the general abbot as their head and the general chapter as their parliament. In the late fifteenth century, the general chapters of Cluny, Cîteaux, Prémontré were vainly striving to assert their authority. Each house claimed a right to dispose of its own property and to select its own members. If visitors are sent, the prior of St. Euverte writes, "they are received at great cost and richly entertained. Neighbors and great personages are invited to come and feast with them, and gold is freely spent to shut their mouths." The same individualistic spirit led the officers in each house to make themselves independent, to rebel against

the old communal spirit of monasticism, and secure for themselves private incomes out of the common property. Thus did monastic offices become real benefices, which often fell into the hands of non-resident seculars. Here again, administrative anarchy led to a general relaxation of discipline, with the worst possible consequences in morals.

We have shown that the main obstacle to reformation in the Church was the complicated entanglement of vested interests. Now, those interests were reducible to terms of money: hence the importance of the financial aspect of the ecclesiastical problems of the time. The clergy needed resources to carry on the various phases of their work, and owing to the disorganized state of the Church, those resources were not forthcoming, or were diverted into other channels. In the case of bishops, these ought to have included the ordinary dues levied on benefices, and the chancery and law fees. But all the exempt bodies, with their dependencies, refused to pay the former; while the latter brought in far less than they ought to have done because so many people withdrew themselves from episcopal jurisdiction. In 1482, the General Chapter of Cluny forbade all the houses of the Order to pay to the bishops the usual duty on their accession to their sees, or the visitation fees. About the same period, many parish priests also claimed exemption from taxes. As a consequence, the exchequer of many sees was in a sad plight. In 1461, the revenue of the archbishopric of Rouen had fallen to the paltry sum of 2000 French livres.

It was no easy task to extend or increase the taxes on benefices; but other duties imposed upon the laity might bring in more, and the bishops turned their efforts that way, from 1450 onward.

A steady effort was made to extract more from marriage fees and the proving of wills. At Paris, in 1505, parish priests would refuse to bury the deceased whose wills had not been proved. Ecclesiastical censures were used freely against those who refused to pay; and in France the evidence of royal officers—even though it should be taken at a discount—throws light upon a stupendous state of affairs. In 1500, in the Clermont diocese, if we are to believe a procurator royal, there were some thirty or forty thousand excommunicated persons. Authentic records show a steady increase at Sens from 1468 to 1505. The dignity of the Church could be no gainer by such a cheapening of her censures; and while in the long run this increased pressure on the part of the clergy did little toward improving their financial position, it paved the way for the Protestant rebellion. In England popular feeling against Church taxation was running high toward 1520; and Henry VIII made use of the leverage thus offered him in his struggle against the Holy See.

The parish clergy was even worse off. Indeed, the churchwardens had considerable resources at their disposal, in the shape both of taxes, bequests, and foundations; but these funds were reserved for the building, repairing, and furnishing of the churches. The priest himself had no claim upon them, and might in most cases be described in Chaucer's words as "a povre persoun of a toun." Here again, the root of the evil lay in the faulty organization of the Church. Lay patronage had been reduced to some extent, but clerical patronage was fast gaining ground. The monasteries or chapters to which benefices were appropriated were entitled to the tithes, on condition that they should provide a decent income for the incumbent; but

in general they proved to be close-fisted, and failed to fulfill their obligations adequately. Parishes, especially in rural areas, were too numerous and too small, and in many cases the priests were literally starving. We hear of some in Normandy living on an income of less than one "sou" a day, only half the pay of an artisan. What wonder, then, that the lower clergy should have made shift as best they could to grind a livelihood out of their parishes? Some took up a trade; most raised the duties for burials and churchings, begged for Masses, quarreled over their revenues with monks or friars, and charged fees for the sacraments.

We have now reached the point where financial maladministration led to religious abuses properly speaking. The doctrinal contentions of the Reformers were, to a large extent, the translation into theological language of a protest against undue payments exacted from the laity. This applied not merely to Church taxation proper, but also to voluntary contributions. Public charity had done beautiful work in building churches, cathedrals and hospitals, roads and bridges, under ecclesiastical supervision. But toward the year 1500, amidst the general confusion which we have described, there was a scramble for alms in which the most objectionable means were used. "Pardoners" often went far beyond the letter of the bulls which authorized them, or even hawked indulgences about without any permission at all. The piety and credulity of the people were exploited by swindlers, who carried about false relics or spurious indulgences. In 1506, the chapter of Soissons imprisoned a cleric who had produced forged bulls, allowing him to beg alms for the ransoming of prisoners; and there are many similar instances. Worse still, the sale of indulgences was pushed by means of unorthodox doctrine, as for instance that "whoever paid into the almsbox for the Crusade a tester for a soul in Purgatory, would free that Soul from Purgatory incontinently."

This abuse of Christian truth was bad enough, but it was not the only moral evil that followed upon the disorganized state of the Church. We have shown how tempting it was for the members of the hierarchy to neglect dioceses in which they met with resistance on every hand, and to join the courts of princes, where their abilities would meet with recognition. Thus in every country of Christian Europe the episcopate became an aristocracy of courtiers. Too much has been made of the serious moral lapses of some of them; but the least that can be said of the others is that they led a brilliant and pleasurable life, far removed from the obligations of their charge. They entrusted the care of their dioceses to deputies and accompanied the sovereign in his wanderings from castle to castle, or even in his campaigns. In the Italian wars, three cardinals, two archbishops, six bishops, and an abbot were in the following of Louis XII of France when he entered Milan in 1507. Some of these took part, with much gusto, in the actual fighting. At a court festival, about the same time, two cardinals danced before the king.

The prelates soon became accustomed to an easy and luxurious life. Cardinal d'Amboise erected a palace at Gaillon, on which he spent no less than 50,000 French livres. Wolsey's residence at Hampton Court immediately suggests itself as an English parallel. Much money was of course needed for the life which was to be led in such surroundings. Each bishop endeavored to obtain a growing number of benefices, and the crying scandal of pluralities became quite general. "The higher clergy," the German Johann Butzbach writes, "are much to blame for the neglect of souls. They send to the parishes unworthy pastors, while they themselves draw the tithes. Many seek to heap up for themselves as many benefices as possible, without fulfilling the duties incumbent upon them, and squander the ecclesiastical revenues in luxury and servants, pages, horses and dogs." That the influence of temporal sovereigns, in attaching to themselves those whose services were due to the Church, was largely responsible for this state of things, cannot be doubted.

The lower clergy had their own reasons for disliking residence in impoverished parishes, where it was impossible for a clever man to "get along" or to proceed with his studies. Toward the end of the fifteenth century, when the archdeacon of Paris was engaged upon a visitation, he found that 36 incumbents out of 83 were nonresident, while 12 had left their cures without permission. Those who supplied their places were the poorest and least qualified of the ecclesiastical body. Indeed, no systematic provision at all was made for the religious training of the parochial clergy as a whole. Some few of them only, who belonged to the gentry or to well-to-do burgher families, were lucky enough to attend a university or a chapter-school. The others had to be content with the teaching given at a village-school, or the lessons of the rector of the parish; they gathered a few scraps of Latin, learned enough theology and liturgy to say Mass, administer the sacraments, bury the dead, and keep the church accounts. They took orders without ever leaving their native place. No effort was made to develop the priestly spirit in their souls. They considered themselves as very much on the same level as their parishioners; and this lack of clerical dignity, coupled with their poverty, caused them to lead the same life, and indulge in the same pleasures, as the common rabble. There is truth indeed in Rabelais' satire of the lower clergy.

With the regulars also, financial and moral decay went hand in hand, the main cause being, here again, administrative abuse. A growing number of religious houses were held *in commendam* by Church dignitaries or members of the aristocracy who considered them merely as sources of income, never visited them, refused to pay for necessary repairs, and reduced them to sore financial straits. In 1486, the monks of Saint-Denis lodged a complaint against their commendatory abbot. The roofs of the church, cloisters, and dorters, they said, let in the rain; most barns and manors were falling to ruin; the scholars of the college which the abbey kept in Paris had been turned out; they themselves were scarcely able to obtain the necessaries of life; the sums allotted for their clothing and wine had been pared down; and their bread was so bad that they could not eat it; all this because the abbot had built extensive lodgings for his own convenience, and granted the benefices "to strangers who let everything melt away." Such a state of things seems to have been quite general and many monasteries were heavily in debt. Financial distress, the spirit of revolt, and relaxed discipline went, of course, hand in hand. To this must be added that the feudal aristocracy had gradually found their way into the religious houses as well as into the hierarchy. Monastic dignities and offices were reserved for the younger sons of noble families. The ideal of equality and common property had therefore disappeared. At Paris, in

1481, during the public festivities of the Epiphany, a number of monks joined with the students, dressed up as fools, armed themselves, and ranged about the city, abusing and attacking the passersby. Women's cloisters were in the same pitiable condition. At le Vergier, it was found in the course of a visitation that the abbey was not closed, that the nuns had not gone to confession for six months, and that the abbess had not received Communion for fifteen months.

Dioceses in which most parishes were in the hands, not of the bishops, but of distant and neglectful patrons; in which exempt bodies of all kinds asserted their independence and spent their time in private quarrels; in which the higher clergy were elegant courtiers, while the lower clergy scarcely managed to live from hand to mouth; financial conditions which resulted in increased taxation for the laity, and the peddling of holy things by ecclesiastical mountebanks; monasteries which refused to submit to the heads of their orders, and in which the offices were held either by non-resident seculars or by disdainful and profligate noblemen, while the monks and nuns were left uncared for materially and spiritually; such is the state of affairs that we are faced with on the eve of the Reformation. The surprising thing, in the circumstances, is not that the level of Christian morality should have been low, but that it should still have been so high. In any case, a general administrative readjustment was needed; but no Church assembly, however holy and well-meaning, could effect it by its own means. Only a powerful central authority would be able to override all the vested interests which were unwilling to let themselves be dislodged.

Now, it was the tragedy of the late

fifteenth and early sixteenth centuries that the papacy was disabled, almost until it was too late, from undertaking the necessary work of reconstruction. Of course the Holy See would have enjoyed greater authority and heightened respect had its moral decay not made it, for a time at least, unworthy of its task; and yet, the very evils and abuses which are most frequently denounced were largely brought about by external causes, over which the popes had no control. The nationalism so prominent at the Council of Constance (1414–1417) asserted itself anew, as the century wore on, in a less democratic shape. The power of national sovereigns was fast becoming absolute, and was attempting to embrace the ecclesiastical province as well. The attention of rulers was focused upon "policy," upon what was purely human and temporal in the government of their states, and they no longer even suspected the necessity of an independent spiritual body. The administration of the Church must be solely in their hands; and the pope must be content with the part of a chaplain, who might be allowed to preach, so long as he did not make himself offensive, but who might not on any account be granted actual powers of government.

Long before such theories were expounded by Bishop Stephen Gardiner as a justification of the Anglican schism, they had been acted upon by most sovereigns in Europe, even in countries which were afterwards to be considered the stanchest supporters of the papacy. In 1498, Spain was threatening to break off its allegiance to the Holy See, and Pope Alexander VI had to placate the Spanish sovereigns by granting them supreme authority over religious affairs within their dominions. Later, in 1508, the Spanish government claimed and obtained full rights of patronage over all churches in the West Indies. France very nearly started a schism of her own at the time of the Council of Pisa, convened by Louis XII (1511–1512). Venice went almost to the same lengths. Not merely did the Signory, in the first decade of the sixteenth century, arraign clerks before its tribunals—the question of clerical immunities being a debatable one—but it went so far as to appoint to benefices and even to bishoprics, not even allowing the pope to withhold confirmation of these acts.

Nor was this struggle to maintain the spiritual independence of the Church the only difficulty that the Holy See had to contend with. Its liberty and the very life of the popes were constantly threatened, in the late fifteenth century, and within the very walls of Rome, by feuds between powerful families, such as the Orsinis and the Colonnas, who wished to have the pope in their dependence. Maintenance of order in the papal dominions, or in the Eternal City itself, was a formidable problem. The nobility of central Italy was unruly and turbulent. The papacy was no better protected against the undertakings of mightier neighbors. France, Spain, the Empire, Venice, all wanted to extend their influence in the Peninsula, nibbled at the patrimony, took cardinals or Roman noblemen in their pay, and raised rebellions against the Holy See. Italy was overrun with foreign armies. In the circumstances, since the papacy had no sufficient military force at its disposal, the only possible policy was to play off the powers against each other, a policy to which Julius II was reduced throughout the length of his pontificate (1503–1513).

Here again, the disorders of the times were reflected in a financial crisis. Huge sums were needed for the administration of the universal Church, and for its defense against the Turkish invasion. The older sources of income had well-nigh dried up. Extensive parts of the patrimony had been usurped by the local nobility; feudal dues, rents, and tributes were not forthcoming, or lost in value through being farmed out. At the end of the fifteenth century, the total produce of customs, salt taxes, and feudal dues amounted to the wholly inadequate sum of 125,000 ducats. There was but one way out of the difficulty, the same one which both parish priests and bishops had taken, and one which was not likely to make the Church popular: namely, to raise the fees which were due to the Holy See for its spiritual services. Apart from tenths, first fruits, and various duties to be paid by the holders of benefices, the fees for dispensations of different kinds were increased 100 percent from 1471 to 1515.

Unfortunately, this oppressive system of taxation, while breeding much discontent, brought in far less than it ought to have done. Sovereigns insisted on retaining their share of all subsidies granted by their clergy to the papacy; the taxpayers took advantage of the fact that as a rule no compulsion was available against them, while tax-collectors, secretaries, and notaries of all descriptions retained for their own use a large part of the sums paid in to them. Two-thirds at least of the assessed moneys never reached the Curia at all. The budget of the Apostolic Chamber, the center of papal administration, had fallen, in the space of sixty years preceding the Reformation, from 300,000 to 150,000 ducats. On the eve of the Reformation, the sum total of all papal revenues amounted only to a maximum of 450,000 ducats, while in such a small kingdom as

Naples, the poll-tax alone brought in 600,000. In 1484, Pope Sixtus IV had to pawn his tiara for 100,000 ducats. From 1471 to 1520 the Holy See was constantly in debt. In fact, it had become impossible to enforce a system of papal taxation throughout Europe, at a time when the ideal of an united Christendom was being battered down by the spirit of nationalism.

The dangers which threatened the independence of the papacy on the one hand, and the financial straits to which it was reduced on the other, account for many of the "abuses" which had crept into the Curia. The position of the popes in the early sixteenth century cannot be compared to what it is nowadays. European public opinion might be devotedly loyal; but distance made it difficult for it to count in Italy, while the papacy was really dependent on the play and counterplay of intrigue and strife between Roman or Florentine factions.

It was impossible for the popes not to engage in that intricate game of local politics; and first of all, they were compelled to recruit a body of faithful adherents, who were not likely to turn traitors. Now, in a country where the ties of blood count for more than any other bond, none were better fitted than the pontiff's own kinsmen to form that bodyguard. Hence arose what has been so often branded as "nepotism"—hence, too, followed even the appointment of juvenile cardinals, whom it was safe to attach to the papal fortunes as early as possible, and who did not always turn out to be scapegraces.

There is less to be said in defense of the sale of ecclesiastical offices, or even cardinals' hats, though this was but one of the makeshifts used by Alexander VI to fill his treasury. At the consistory of May 31, 1503, nine cardinals were appointed, "most of them men of slender reputation." Some of them had paid up to 20,000 ducats and more, the total sum received amounting to 130,000 ducats. Such simony, however, still failed its purpose. Sixtus IV, Alexander VI, Julius II, and even Leo X, were compelled to have recourse to bankers. In 1513, the debt of Leo X to some of these rose to 125,000 ducats. Since the bankers—such as the Medici at Florence, the Dorias at Genoa, the Fuggers at Augsburg—naturally enough wanted pledges, permission was given to their local branches to collect the papal taxes directly. They even acted as intermediate agents between suitors for papal exemptions, dispensations, or benefices, and the Holy See. Thus there arose a huckstering in properly religious favors, which could only be detrimental to the good name of the Church.

The situation was the same in regard to the head of the Church as to her limbs. The times were changing. A system of administration, which had been possible and satisfactory as long as Europe was spiritually united under the authority of the Holy See, ceased to work once the disruptive spirit of lay statecraft gained the upper hand. The worst of it was that the papacy itself, being compelled to act less as an universal spiritual power than as a second-rate Italian principality, became infected by the new spirit, that of the pagan Renaissance, and tended to model itself on temporal courts. Thus moral evils arose, which cannot be excused or justified. In fact, however, the most scandalous period was not of very long duration, since it coincided with the pontificate of Alexander VI, which lasted from 1492 to 1503. But the condition of the papal court at the time might well give rise to righteous indignation. The pope show-

ered favors upon his children, especially on Caesar Borgia; and the worst instance of his paternal generosity is the lavish way in which he granted to his son, who needed much money for his campaigns toward the enlargement of his dominions, much of the sums brought in by the jubilee of 1500. Beside such a misuse of the pope's power and such a betrayal of the trust shown to him by the pilgrims, common immorality will fall almost flat. Yet one imagines the impression produced on pious foreigners by such events as the solemn festivities for the second wedding of Alexander VI's daughter, Lucrece Borgia, one of the shows consisting in licentious dances, at which the pope himself was a spectator.

The moral level of the Roman court was much higher during the following pontificate, that of Julius II; nepotism disappeared, and the revenues of the Holy See were no longer squandered. But administrative and financial malpractices were not discontinued. The same old means were used to fill the papal treasury: the sale of offices, of benefices, of indulgences. Ecclesiastical censures were being constantly used for temporal purposes such as the recovery of Bologna from the Venetians.

In short, the same thing had happened to the Church which happens to most human societies. Without any deliberate evil intentions on the part of anyone, abuses creep in, which are gradually sanctioned by conservative habits and become almost respectable through age. They no longer give rise to wonderment or protest, and things are allowed to glide down the slope of perdition, the more comfortably, as so many vested interests would suffer if a root-and-branch reformation were undertaken. Only a man of uncommon sanctity, enthusiasm, and clearsightedness is able to cope with such a state of things; and in fact it did take a good many such men to plan a new organization for the Church, and keep her abreast of the times. They could hardly have succeeded, however, had Christendom been really corrupt at heart; but it was not. The material was lying ready for the hand of the builders: Christian Europe was rich in faith, charity, and devotion.

PRESERVED SMITH (1880–1941), who for many years greatly influenced American interpretations of the Reformation, came from a New England family and was educated at Amherst College and Columbia University, where he received his Ph.D. in 1907. After teaching for a time at Harvard University he went to Cornell in 1922, where he remained as professor of history for the rest of his life. One of his first publications was *Letters of Martin Luther* (1911), but probably his most important work was *The Age of the Reformation* (1920), in which he sought to set forth a basically nontheological interpretation of the movement.*

▶ # *Changes in Scientific Knowledge and Ethical Feeling*

The reader will expect me, after having given some account of the estimates of others, to make an evaluation of my own. Of course no view can be final; mine, like that of everyone else, is the expression of an age and an environment as well as that of an individual.

The Reformation, like the Renaissance and the sixteenth-century Social Revolution, was but the consequence of the operation of antecedent changes in environment and habit, intellectual and economic. There was the widening and deepening of knowledge, due in one aspect to the invention of printing, in the other to the geographical and historical discoveries of the fifteenth century and the consequent adumbration of the idea of natural law. Even in the later schoolmen, like Biel and Occam, still more in the humanists, one finds a much stronger rationalism than in the representative thinkers of the Middle Ages. The general economic antecedent was the growth in wealth and the change in the system of production from gild and barter to that of money and wages. This produced three secondary results, which in turn operated as causes: the rise of the moneyed class, individualism, and nationalism.

All these tendencies, operating in three fields, the religious, the political and the intellectual, produced the Ref-

* From *The Age of the Reformation* by Preserved Smith. Copyright 1920 by Holt, Rinehart and Winston, Inc. Copyright 1948 by Preserved Smith. Reprinted by permission of Holt, Rinehart and Winston, Inc. Pp. 743–750.

ormation and its sisters, the Renaissance and the Social Revolution of the sixteenth century. The Reformation—including in that term both the Protestant movement and the Catholic reaction—partly occupied all these fields, but did not monopolize any of them. There were some religious, or anti-religious, movements outside the Reformation, and the Lutheran impulse swept into its own domain large tracts of the intellectual and political fields, primarily occupied by Renaissance and Revolution.

(1) The *gêne* felt by many secular historians in the treatment of religion is now giving way to the double conviction of the importance of the subject and of its susceptibility to scientific study. Religion in human life is not a subject apart, nor is it necessary to regard all theological revolts as obscurantist. As a rationalist has remarked, it is usually priests who have freed mankind from taboos and superstitions. Indeed, in a religious age, no effective attack on the existing church is possible save one inspired by piety.

Many instructive parallels to the Reformation can be found both in Christian history and in that of other religions; they all markedly show the same consequences of the same causes. The publication of Christianity, with its propaganda of monotheism against the Roman world and its accentuation of faith against the ceremonialism of the Jewish church, resembled that of Luther's "gospel." Marcion with his message of Pauline faith and his criticism of the Bible, was a second-century Reformer. The iconoclasm and nationalism of the Emperor Leo furnish striking similarities to the Protestant Revolt. The movements started by the medieval mystics and still more by the heretics Wyclif and Huss, rehearsed the religious drama of the six-teenth century. Many revivals in the Protestant church, such as Methodism, were, like the original movement, returns to personal piety and biblicism. The Old Catholic schism in its repudiation of the papal supremacy, and even Modernism, notwithstanding its disclaimers, are animated in part by the same motives as those inspiring the Reformers. In Judaism the Sadducees, in their bibliolatry and in their opposition to the traditions dear to the Pharisees, were Protestants; a later counterpart of the same thing is found in the reform the Karaites by Anan ben David. Mohammed has been a favorite subject for comparison with Luther by the Catholics, but in truth, in no disparaging sense, the proclamation of Islam, with its monotheism, emphasis on faith and predestination, was very like the Reformation, and so were several later reforms within Mohammedanism, including two in the sixteenth century. Many parallels could doubtless be adduced from the heathen religions, perhaps the most striking is the foundation of Sikhism by Luther's contemporary Nanak, who preached monotheism and revolted from the ancient ceremonial and hierarchy of caste.

What is the etiology of religious revolution? The principal law governing it is that any marked change either in scientific knowledge or in ethical feeling necessitates a corresponding alteration in the faith. All the great religious innovations of Luther and his followers can be explained as an attempt to readjust faith to the new culture, partly intellectual, partly social, that had gradually developed during the later Middle Ages.

The first shift, and the most important, was that from salvation by works to salvation by faith only. The Catholic dogma is that salvation is dependent on certain sacraments, grace being bestowed automatically (*ex opere operato*) on all who participate in the celebration of the rite without actively opposing its effect. Luther not only reduced the number of sacraments but he entirely changed their character. Not they, but the faith of the participant mattered, and this faith was bestowed freely by God, or not at all. In this innovation one primary cause was the individualism of the age; the sense of the worth of the soul or, if one pleases, of the ego. This did not mean subjectivism, or religious autonomy, for the Reformers held passionately to an ideal of objective truth, but it did mean that every soul had the right to make its personal account with God, without mediation of priest or sacrament. Another element in this new dogma was the simpler, and yet more profound, psychology of the new age. The shift of emphasis from the outer to the inner is traceable from the earliest age to the present, from the time when Homer delighted to tell of the good blows struck in fight to the time when fiction is but the story of an inner, spiritual struggle. The Reformation was one phase in this long process from the external to the internal. The debit and credit balance of outward work and merit was done away, and for it was substituted the nobler, or at least more spiritual and less mechanical, idea of disinterested morality and unconditioned salvation. The God of Calvin may have been a tyrant, but he was not corruptible by bribes.

We are so much accustomed to think of dogma as the *esse* of religion that it is hard for us to do justice to the importance of this change. Really, it is not dogma so much as rite and custom that is fundamental. The sacramental habit of mind was common to medieval Christianity and to most primitive religions. For the first time Luther substituted for the sacramental habit, or attitude, its antithesis, an almost purely ethical criterion of faith. The transcendental philosophy and the categorical imperative lay implicit in the famous *sola fide*.

The second great change made by Protestantism was more intellectual, that from a pluralistic to a monistic standpoint. Far from the conception of natural law, the early Protestants did little or nothing to rationalize, or explain away, the creeds of the Catholics, but they had arrived at a sufficiently monistic philosophy to find scandal in the worship of the saints, with its attendant train of daily and trivial miracles. To sweep away the vast hierarchy of angels and canonized persons that made Catholicism quasi-polytheistic, and to preach pure monotheism was in the spirit of the time and is a phenomenon for which many parallels can be found. Instructive is the analogy of the contemporary trend to absolutism; neither God nor king any longer needed intermediaries.

(2) In two aspects the Reformation was the religious expression of the current political and economic change. In the first place it reflected and reacted upon the growing national self-consciousness, particularly of the Teutonic peoples. The revolt from Rome was in the interests of the state church, and also of Germanic culture. The break-up of the Roman church at the hands of the Northern peoples is strikingly like the break-up of the Roman Empire under pressure from their ancestors. Indeed, the limits of the Roman church practically coincided with the boundaries of the Empire. The apparent exception of England proves the rule, for in Britain the Roman civilization was swept away

by the German invasions of the fifth and following centuries.

That the Reformation strengthened the state was inevitable, for there was no practical alternative to putting the final authority in spiritual matters, after the pope had been ejected, into the hands of the civil government. Congregationalism was tried and failed as tending to anarchy. But how little the Reformation was really responsible for the new despotism and the divine right of kings, is clear from a comparison with the Greek church and the Turkish Empire. In both, the same forces which produced the state churches of Western Europe operated in the same way. Selim I, a bigoted Sunnite, after putting down the Shi'ite heresy, induced the last caliph of the Abbasid dynasty to surrender the sword and mantle of the prophet; thereafter he and his successors were caliphs as well as sultans. In Russia Ivan the Terrible made himself, in 1547, head of the national church.

Protestantism also harmonized with the capitalistic revolution in that its ethics are, far more than those of Catholicism, oriented by a reference to this world. The old monastic ideal of celibacy, solitude, mortification of the flesh, prayer and meditation, melted under the sun of a new prosperity. In its light men began to realize the ethical value of this life, of marriage, of children, of daily labor and of success and prosperity. It was just in this work that Protestantism came to see its chance of serving God and one's neighbor best. The man at the plough, the maid with the broom, said Luther, are doing God better service than does the praying, self-tormenting monk.

Moreover, the accentuation of the virtues of thrift and industry, which made capitalism and Calvinism allies, but reflected the standards natural to the bourgeois class. It was by the might of the merchants and their money that the Reformation triumphed; conversely they benefited both by the spoils of the church and by the abolition of a privileged class. Luther stated that there was no difference between priest and layman; some men were called to preach, others to make shoes, but—and this is his own illustration—the one vocation is no more spiritual than the other. No longer necessary as a mediator and dispenser of sacramental grace, the Protestant clergyman sank inevitably to the same level as his neighbors.

(3) In its relation to the Renaissance and to modern thought the Reformation solved, in its way, two problems, or one problem, that of authority, in two forms. Though anything but consciously rational in their purpose, the innovating leaders did assert, at least for themselves, the right of private judgment. Appealing from indulgence-seller to pope, from pope to council, from council to the Bible and (in Luther's own words) from the Bible to Christ, the Reformers finally came to their own conscience as the supreme court. Trying to deny to others the very rights they had fought to secure for themselves, yet their example operated more powerfully than their arguments, even when these were made of ropes and of thumb-screws. The delicate balance of faith was overthrown and it was put into a condition of unstable equilibrium; the avalanche, started by ever so gentle a push, swept onward until it buried the men who tried to stop it half way. Dogma slowly narrowing down from precedent to precedent had its logical, though unintended, outcome in complete religious autonomy, yes, in infidelity and skepticism.

Protestantism has been represented

now as the ally, now as the enemy of humanism. Consciously it was neither. Rather, it was the vulgarization of the Renaissance; it transformed, adapted, and popularized many of the ideas originated by its rival. It is easy to see now that the future lay rather outside of both churches than in either of them, if we look only for direct descent. Columbus burst the bounds of the world, Copernicus those of the universe; Luther only broke his vows. But the point is that the repudiation of religious vows was the hardest to do at that time, a feat infinitely more impressive to the masses than either of the former. It was just here that the religious movement became a great solvent of conservatism; it made the masses think, passionately if not deeply, on their own beliefs. It broke the cake of custom and made way for greater emancipations than its own. It was the logic of events that, whereas the Renaissance gave freedom of thought to the cultivated few, the Reformation finally resulted in tolerance for the masses. Logically also, even while it feared and hated philosophy in the great thinkers and scientists, it advocated education, up to a certain point, for the masses.

In summary, if the Reformation is judged with historical imagination, it does not appear to be primarily a reaction. That it should be such is both *a priori* improbable and unsupported by the facts. The Reformation did not give *our* answer to the many problems it was called upon to face; nevertheless it gave the solution demanded and accepted by the time, and therefore historically the valid solution. With all its limitations it was, fundamentally, a step forward and not the return to an earlier standpoint, either to that of primitive Christianity, as the Reformers themselves claimed, or to the dark ages, as has been latterly asserted.

EVA PRIESTER, born in St. Petersburg, now
Leningrad, in 1910, has gained a considerable
reputation as a Marxist historian and journalist in
eastern Europe. She began her journalistic career
with the *Berliner Tageblatt,* but has contributed to
a large number of Marxist-oriented periodicals. The
work from which this selection is taken is her
interpretation of Austrian history, and it presents
very clearly the Marxist view of the Reformation. In
the introduction she explains that since she wrote
the book in England during World War II, she was
unable to consult Russian histories, which would no
doubt have ensured her keeping strictly to the party
line.*

► *A Socio-economic Phenomenon*

The remodeling of European society
between the fifteenth and the seventeenth
centuries was brought about by means of
severe crises not only in the political
but also in the religious, or what is better described as the ecclesiastical, arena.
The Church was a part of the social ap-
paratus in every country, and like all
other institutions of the age it was subject to change during the transition from
the rule of the feudal aristocracy to
absolutism.

In nearly all the lands of Europe occurred what has been summarized under
the name Reformation: the evolution of
a new form of church which no longer
came under a supranational authority
(the Pope) but rather under secular au-

thority (the king in England, the princes
in Germany, the towns in Switzerland
and the Netherlands). But only some of
the European nations broke completely
with Catholicism. While the Reformation was still at its height, the Counter-
Reformation, the struggle to create a
Church which while remaining Catholic
would nevertheless in practice be dependent on the (ruling) dynasties, had
already begun in certain countries—
France, Spain, Austria. Austria was one
of the countries where the Reformation
at first made extraordinary progress. By
the middle of the sixteenth century more
than half the inhabitants of the country
were Protestant and in some areas as
many as 80 percent. After a short period

*Reprinted from Eva Priester, *Kurze Geschichte Österreichs* (Vienna: Globus-Buchvertrieb,
1946), pp. 111–119. Translated by C. J. Munford and W. Stanford Reid.

of "compromise Catholicism," the attempt to create a new form of the Church in which Lutheranism and Catholicism would mingle, the era of the Counter-Reformation began. By the middle of the seventeenth century this period had come to an end; Austria had once again become almost 100 percent Catholic.

This development unfolded in severe struggles, accompanied by revolts, civil wars, and the expulsion of thousands of people from their country. Finally it moved into the great European showdown of the Thirty Years' War, constituting one of its elements.

Why had the Catholic Church, which had once been a great civilizing force and had formed an important part of the social structure for many long centuries, now become intolerable in its old form for nearly all of Europe? Why was Austria which owed a great part of its economic and spiritual development to Scottish monks and the Benedictines, to the lords of the monasteries of Meld and Salzburg, also shaken by the great battle between the Reformed and old church?

The political conflict of the Reformation had several causes. During the Middle Ages the Church was the only force able to fulfill the functions which we today call cultural and social work. It provided the officials for administration in positions that did not have to do directly with war and required a certain amount of knowledge—financial administration, legal affairs, care of the aged, schools, care of orphans, medicine, and so forth. It was indispensable to any land in which even half-orderly conditions were to prevail, and to any prince who wished to rule his country in fact as well as in name. It was not subordinate to the local lord, but was instead a supranational corporation with its central seat in Rome. Under the loose system of feudalism in which no firm central authority existed, such a state of affairs was certainly possible. In those countries where even before the modern era there were relatively powerful territorial lords, the princes from early times had to establish a certain measure of control over the Church. In Austria the struggle for acquisition by the local lords of part of the Church revenues—which except for amounts needed by the local church went to Rome—began under the Babenbergs and became more intense under the Habsburgs. At a very early date and without open conflict with the Pope, the chronically impoverished Habsburgs were able to appropriate a certain portion of the Church revenues. Furthermore, in the fourteenth century, they halted the accumulation of landed property by Austrian monasteries and charitable institutions, for example, forbidding the burghers of the towns to give or will land to the Church without the express consent of either the municipal council or the territorial ruler. But those were only minor skirmishes.

The development of early capitalism, the rise of the absolute state, and the beginning of national development altered the entire position of the Church. As an economic and cultural force the Church became to a considerable extent superfluous. The towns gradually took over all social welfare. In Austria this development was most obvious in Vienna. The guilds took the place of the Church, which had cared for the sick and the aged, raised orphans, and maintained schools. They established their own homes for the elderly and hospitals and even created certain types of social insurance and pensions for their members. In some areas, the Tyrol for example, the estates (*Stände*) also assumed part of the social and cultural functions of the Church. In the middle of the sixteenth century the Tyrolese estates carried out a full-scale school reform. The monastic schools were replaced by provincial schools (*Landesschulen*), whose pedagogical principles were for that time extraordinarily modern. The curriculum consisted of five subjects: reading, writing, arithmetic, religion, and song. Teachers were advised to abstain from the use of "fists and hair-pulling." A priest and two secular state officials supervised the schools. However, since the new schools were secondary and higher educational establishments, there was still no universal compulsory attendance.

From Chancellor to scribe, from judge to physician, the Church in the Middle Ages provided all the functionaries for the machinery of public administration, for the physical and intellectual welfare of the population. Since neither nobility nor peasantry nor the then very weak urban middle class were able to produce men for these occupations, a stratum of intellectuals and officials outside the Church grew up only very slowly. The sons of rich burghers, occasionally some well-to-do peasants, and some members of the impoverished knights' estate began to devote themselves to administration and the liberal professions. Some did this voluntarily and others, especially the nobility, to escape complete pauperization. The great physician and chemist Paracelsus (1493–1541), who although he was born in Switzerland lived in Austria from early childhood and later worked there, was a representative of the new secular intelligentsia. Another was Siegmund von Herberstein, whose description of conditions in Russia (*Rerum Moscoviticarum Commentarii*, 1549) constituted one of the most important contemporary standard works on Russia. There were numerous laymen among the members of what was then the University of Vienna and among the humanists of the Danubischen Gesellschaft (Danube Society).

From the moment when a national officialdom subordinate to the provincial lord began to take shape, the public machinery of the Church, dependent on Rome or on non-Austrian prelates, became an encumbrance. Like an independent, self-sufficient nobility, a self-sufficient, independent church hindered and complicated the process of centralization. Like the former it became a state within the state and thus a threat to absolutism. In addition the head of the Church, the Pope, had long since shed the pretence of neutrality, becoming an Italian prince and alternating between a pro-Austrian and pro-French policy. Thus over and over again an element opposed to the interests of the country was drawn into Austrian—or into French—domestic affairs. In both countries the situation was equally intolerable.

The financial structure of the Church, through which part of Church revenues were sent abroad, came into conflict with the rising national economy. It was precisely the urban middle class which from the beginning of the sixteenth century constantly and openly complained that "good money is going to Rome so that the Pope can build churches and palaces there." Not only for the lower urban middle class but also for the great merchant capitalists—especially in Spain, France, and England—the Church became a force that hindered rather than helped. The moral outlook of the Church was medieval; it represented an age when it had attained its zenith and no longer corresponded to the present.

The flowering of the Church had taken place in an era during which slavery, then a hindrance to the further development of the society, had been replaced by serfdom and bondage. The Church therefore was not against serfdom but it was resolutely against slavery. Consequently, it bitterly opposed the traders and conquerors who engaged in a brisk slave trade in the newly discovered areas of Africa and South America, thus laying the foundation for their great wealth. It fought them with sermons, papal prescriptions, and even the threat of exclusion from the Church. Having come into being in an age when a money economy hardly existed and thus having little need for gold and silver, the Church found it difficult to understand the sudden hunger for gold that now seized all of Europe. It thus came out sharply against the conquerors of South America and the Spanish slave traders in North Africa who slaughtered thousands of natives or who, in order to force out gold and silver, drove them to work the mines under inhuman conditions. In this period the Church often protected native inhabitants from European conquerors, contending that as soon as they were baptized they acquired the same rights as Europeans. But finally the Church, which economically was a part of the landowning aristocracy—the bishops and prelates in Austria and in other countries were in practice great nobles and carried out the same policies as their lay colleagues—was affected by the same process of moral decay as the rest of the historically obsolete class of the nobility. The amorous adventures of monks and nuns and the venality of high ecclesiastics were at that time proverbial.

Indeed in German depictions of the Reform movement and in those influenced by concepts of "Greater Germany,"[1] this aspect of the matter is given undue emphasis. When one reads such portrayals, especially of the German Reformation, one has the impression that the whole German people were thrown into a panic by the sudden discovery of the moral degeneration of the Church and that it fell as one man into Luther's arms. Thus we must assume that a country in which there were Electors who every day lay drunk in the gutters of their provincial capitals (*Residenzstädte*), a land in which every second Elector's marriage scandals were common topics of discussion in Europe and whose princes openly sold the imperial dignity to the highest bidder, had now hardened its heart against fornication and corruption. In fact, the clerical aristocracy was neither more nor less corrupt than the secular aristocracy, and the morality of the monasteries, which had ceased to be specially advanced units of production, was neither better nor worse than that of many knights' residences. But in the general dissatisfaction with the Church, in the feeling that it was an institution which had outlived its purpose and had became superfluous in its old form, this factor played a certain part.

The Reformation had already occurred before 1517, the year in which Luther nailed his theses to the Church in Wittenberg and in which the dispute concerning the sale of Papal indulgences in Germany exploded into a great Europe-wide Church conflict. For hun-

[1] The author is apparently referring here to those German historians of the nineteenth century who advocated the establishment of a unified German state that might include Austria, but who felt that the Roman Catholic Church was the great obstacle to such unification. They sometimes maintained that Luther's revolt was the first step in the process of forming the "Greater Germany."—Ed.

dreds of years the Church had been shored up: attempts had been made to rejuvenate it through partial reforms and through the foundation of new orders, for example the Franciscans. Hus and his supporters had made the first serious attempt to give nationally advanced Bohemia its own state church. In Austria, too, there had been attempts at reform. At the time of the Hussites, there arose a Hussite movement in Vienna and other Austrian towns which was forcibly suppressed by the Habsburgs. Among the Viennese humanists, there was constant talk of renovating the church "in head and members." Eventually, in 1499, a preacher at St. Stephen's Cathedral proposed theses that were almost word for word the same as Luther's. The reform movement which finally came in 1517 roared like a cyclone through all of Europe.

What made it irresistible was the fact that at the outset all sections of the population—including the crown—were interested in Protestantism, although for differing reasons. The princes—provincial rulers as well as the upper and lower nobility, expected a strengthening of their economic and political power both from the transference of Church estates to their possession (secularization) and from the decline of the moral authority of the Church. The middle class anticipated a new church in closer conformity with their economic and cultural needs than the old one. Lastly, the peasants looked forward to their *own* church, no longer the church of foreign rulers.

For the peasants, the Church—divine service, sermons—was always the most important factor in their lives, their only intellectual activity. But the new, emancipated peasant wanted a church which belonged to him, which spoke his language (no longer Latin), and whose preachers he could choose instead of having to accept them at the behest of a bishop. He wanted a church not compromised for him as before by close relations with the aristocracy. That is why Protestantism in Austria made such progress among the peasants.

Inasmuch as every section of the population had a different understanding of the term church reform, it took very different courses in the various countries, according to which social force was especially influential in a given land. The reform of the Church in Europe developed along three different lines.

In Switzerland, the Netherlands, and some northern towns, everywhere that the middle class was especially strong or the nobility extraordinarily weak, it took the form of Calvinism, which was similar to the Presbyterianism of the Puritans in the English Revolution of the seventeenth century. Calvinism and the forms of religion related to it were essentially of the towns, bourgeois forms of religion. Church administration and structure were closely tied to the administration and structure of the municipality. The conscious and emphatic simplicity of the Calvinists, the sharp rejection of magnificent living quarters and luxurious garb, of excessive joy in life and exaggerated intellectual freedom, their constant emphasis upon the necessity for hard work and a thrifty life were in tune with the economic needs of the advanced urban middle class. The free election of clergymen, the strong democracy in church affairs, accorded with its political needs. The black suits and white collars of the Puritans were a demonstration of the new middle class simplicity and thrift, in contrast to the extravagance of the greater and lesser princes—a demonstration of the busy bees against the drones. To be sure, it was more a religion of the small and middle urban bourgeoisie. A large number of the Continental merchant capitalists had little sympathy for the modest savings of the workers; they made their fortunes more rapidly and in league with the great monarchs, who from the standpoint of the Calvinists were almost more annoying than the nobility.

The second form was Protestantism,[2] the "religion of the Princes," in which the provincial lord, and he alone, was the supreme head of the Church. He held complete power not only over the lives and deaths of his subjects but over their consciences as well. This authority extended so far that finally the territorial ruler acquired the right not only to control the Church but also to determine which religion his subjects could and could not exercise.

Protestantism had completely contrary effects in the various countries. Where there already was a central authority based on the support of the middle class, as in the England of Henry VIII or in Sweden, it strengthened the power of the king, accelerated centralization, and furthered national development. In these countries the Reformation was progressive, even revolutionary. Where there were several strong rulers, it strengthened centrifugal forces because it rendered not one but several princes so much more powerful that their subjugation to a central authority now become impossible. This was the case primarily in Germany. During the age of the Reformation power slipped from the hands of the approximately three hundred princes, towns, and middle nobles who ruled Germany into the hands of a

dozen princes who were much stronger and more dangerous than their predecessors. There arose large and comparatively powerful principalities: Brandenburg, Saxony, Hesse, the Palatinate. These provinces were already a force to be reckoned with and with them it was already profitable to conclude alliances. This had two consequences: henceforth Germany's neighbors—France, Austria, later Sweden and Denmark, and still later England—sought to draw various German princes into their camps and to exploit them for their own purposes. This further strengthened German decentralization, for the German princes were certainly powerful enough to be used, but not powerful enough to use their protagonists seriously for the purposes of their own German national policy. The disintegration of Germany into Austrian, French, Danish, Swedish, English, and Spanish spheres of influence dates from the age of the Reformation.

In France and Austria, however, where the ruling dynasties were victorious but the power of the nobility not broken, Protestantism rapidly became a weapon of the nobility, who were temporarily strengthened by secularization in their revived struggle against the sovereigns. There the Reformation led to a new flare-up of combats of the princely *fronde*. Matters were further complicated by the situation in Germany. Although the German princes were not strong enough to carry out their own policies successfully and to prevent the intervention of foreign powers in Germany, they were powerful enough to be allies not only of the monarchs but also of the nobles who opposed the monarchs. From the middle of the sixteenth century, the Protestant nobility of Austria, as well as of France, sought to strengthen their position against the crown by al-

---

2 The term Protestantism is used here for Lutheranism.—*Ed.*

liances with German Protestant princes. At the same time, by union with those rebellious nobles, the German princes sought either to weaken the Habsburgs, Valois, and Bourbons alike or to force concessions from them. In Austria matters were even more complicated due to the fact that France—still the great rival of the Habsburgs and allied with the Austrian nobility, German Protestants, and Bohemian aristocracy—played at being the European protector of the Protestants, which of course did not prevent it from mercilessly suppressing its own Protestant *fronde*. Piquancy was added to the situation when now and then France succeeded in having *its own* pope elected, and he was also to be found in this French Protestant, German Protestant, Austrian combination.

In a short time this concatenation of all European conflicts and combinations led to an intolerable situation. Every internal dispute led to conflict among the European powers. Every struggle of the Austrian crown against its own (or later against the Bohemian) aristocracy became a latent European war. But was this conflict in any way necessary—at least in the religious sphere? Would it not have been simpler for the rulers of France, Austria, and Spain to become Protestant in order to strengthen their own power, as Henry VIII had done, and at the same time weaken the Protestant *fronde*? It appears that especially for the strong Continental dynasties this road was not accessible.

Franz Mehring noted that the Reformation was by no means an advantageous solution for all countries. The rulers of the economically and politically backward countries, primarily the German princes, needed the Reformation; it was their only means of increasing their power, and they had nothing to

lose from a break with Rome—that is, with Italy. Some of the advanced Continental dynasties did, however, have something to lose from the Reformation. A large part of their economy was still oriented toward Italy and the Mediterranean. A separation from Italy would have had disastrous consequences for their trade and whole economic life. For example, it is significant that the great merchant capitalists, such as the German Fuggers, supported the Catholic side—the Emperor and Bavaria—in the period of struggle against the Reformation; it is said of Fugger that at the height of the Protestant-Catholic conflict, when due to lack of funds Charles V threatened him with concessions to the Protestants, he tore up and threw into the fire the bill for the huge amount that the emperor had borrowed from him. It is also remarkable that such humanists as Erasmus of Rotterdam, or Melanchthon, who had bitterly criticized the Catholic Church, steadily opposed the Protestant schism and favored a compromise with Rome. They too did not wish to cut themselves off completely from Italy, the land of the flourishing Renaissance.

That certainly was not true of all the nations of Europe. For England, Sweden, and Holland, countries which were hardly involved in the trade of the Mediterranean and whose economic development was oriented toward the Atlantic, separation from Italy not only involved no risk but was a necessity. They completed the Reformation quickly and almost without hesitation.

Furthermore, England, Sweden and Holland were not interested in Italy politically, or at least very little. Austria, France, and Spain were in a different position, being rivals in Italy. According to the custom of the age, they fought to bring persons and princely factions to their side, and they fought especially bitterly to win the greatest Italian prince, the Pope. At every papal election the cardinals stood under the concentrated fire of French and Austro-Spanish attempts to influence the outcome. Sometimes the influence was in the form of hard cash. Official and unofficial envoys of all three powers, agents, and spies filled the place in which the election took place. A state that had severed all ties with the Church and publicly joined the Protestant camp would automatically have been excluded from the contest— and thus most likely from Italian politics. For Austria, the threat of Turkish incursion was added. The Popes were indeed uninterested and sometimes even directly allied with the Turks, but at times of great distress it was still possible by means of European public opinion to bring pressure to bear on them and to extort from them a minimum of aid— some funds, a few soldiers, or at least an appeal to Christianity for the defense of menaced Austria. In the straits in which Austria found itself, all help was worthwhile no matter how small.

Although Holland was greatly influenced by the Reformation both religiously and politically, and many Dutchmen have written on the subject, some have not accepted the view that the Reformation possessed great importance. Among the latter is H. A. E. VAN GELDER (b. 1891). A teacher educated at the University of Amsterdam, he has instructed in schools of Sneek, Rotterdam, Breda, and The Hague. By his writings he has also gained a reputation as a historian and has served on the editorial staff of *Tijdschrift voor Geschiedenis* (The Historical Review). He has set forth his views on the Reformation in a number of books: *Revolutionaire Reformatie* (1943); *Erasmus, schilders en rederijkers* (1959) but his most explicit statement appears in *The Two Reformations of the 16th Century*, from which the following selection comes.*

The Renaissance:
The True Reformation

Discussion about the religious importance of Humanism and the Renaissance centred, for a long time, on the question of whether they were Christian or pagan. The answer in most cases used to be that Renaissance man was pagan in outlook, at least (or in particular) in Italy, up to the second quarter of the sixteenth century, although a Christian or biblical Humanism was recognized North of the Alps. After Jacob Burckhardt had written his famous book, the limits of the Renaissance were extended to include much of the Middle Ages. In recent times, however, most scholars have argued that Renaissance men, even in Italy, were more religious than the great Swiss historian had assumed. "Religious," or "believing," was then identified with "Christian," and instead of the opposition of "Christian" and "pagan," a contrast was drawn between "religious" and "irreligious," or "faith" and "incredulity." As far as the Italians were concerned, "Christian" was simply defined as "bearing allegiance to the Catholic creed," or such general distinctions were made as between a "Christian" and a "natural" conception of the world, or "seeing the creation from the point of view of God," and from that of man, opposing a traditional to a rational viewpoint. In particular, the period as a whole, or separate writers in it, were qualified as being individualistic by contrast to the Middle Ages. Never, as far as

* Reprinted from H. A. E. van Gelder, *The Two Reformations of the 16th Century* (The Hague: Martinus Nijhoff, N.V. Publishers of The Hague, 1961), pp. 3–10. Footnotes omitted.

I can see, was the question raised whether it is possible for a person to carry out his religious duties and testify his allegiance to the Church, and nevertheless to hold quite a different opinion about the meaning of these observances and dogmas. None of the scholars has shown that he had a clear view of the fact that religion is not only an attitude to life and the world, but in the first place a confession of faith in specific dogmas, sacraments and ceremonies. It is my view that the religious problem of the Renaissance is not solved by stating that the period was in the main religious or irreligious, Christian or pagan; nor even that its outstanding authors were "Catholic" or belonged to some other "ism." We must ask what meaning each of them attached to such conceptions as revelation, faith, grace, salvation, sanctification, etc., or what value they attached to penance, the eucharist, baptism and the other sacraments.

This will be the first question to be answered here. The answer includes an answer to the problem of Christianity and paganism in the Renaissance. It will be apparent how much the main bearers of Renaissance culture, in Italy as elsewhere, considered themselves to be good Christians, not in the orthodox sense, but as confessors of a Christianity which differs greatly from the faith of the mediaeval Church, and in various ways stands just as close to our "modern" views as did formerly the philosophy of the very highly developed Greeks and Romans.

The problem of the religious views of Renaissance man is closely related to the further problem of the relationship between the Renaissance and the Reformation. In most cases this relationship has been considered chronologically, the Renaissance preceding the Reformation as a period. Sometimes the relationship is seen as a contrast in nature: the Renaissance is regarded as important for the plastic arts, literature, philosophy and philology (with the two latter we speak of Humanism); while the Reformation, on the other hand, is said to have been a religious movement. In works concerned with the history of religion and the churches, a certain amount of attention has also been given to the second period of the Renaissance, which in most cases means the "Christian Humanism" outside Italy. This Humanism is then described as a movement which aimed at a more spiritual view of doctrine and worship, which was directed against abuses in the Church, and against what was termed "popular belief which had degenerated into superstition." Thus Humanists were said to have desired only a *purification* of the Church and not its *reformation*. A real religious revolution, an *Umwertung aller religiösen Werte*, is always said to have first arisen through the "enlivening act" of Luther, and the writings of the Humanists to have served merely to a certain extent as a preparation for this. Religiously speaking, Luther first (and later Calvin) would have carried out and ventured upon the consequences of what had merely been ushered in by Erasmus.

According to Wernle, what was in the mind of some Humanists amounted at the most to a *Reform-Katholicismus*. In this way of thinking Northern or biblical Humanists were forerunners of the Reformation, while on the other side of the Alps disbelief and heathenism were the order of the day, except for some, such as Marsilio Ficino, who is said to have returned to the (Christian) faith in the end, and Pico, who is said to have re-embraced his faith under Savonarola's castigating words. Erasmus and many others in the North are considered more religious, however, and as the real "forerunners of the Reformation," which is described as a more radical movement than Humanism. But as soon as the Reformation got under way, these rapidly turned their backs on it and most joined the Catholic camp. Humanism then, apparently, lost its religious importance. The dispute, according to the normal view, was continued between Protestants and Catholics, and between the various Protestant sects. The "confessional age," as Hans Baron calls it, had begun, and the Renaissance was a closed period, while Humanism survived only in philology and literature. It is generally said that the sixteenth century is the century of the Reformation. If it is desired to credit both the Renaissance and the Reformation with an important role in the development of modern man, it is almost always the latter that is mentioned when religious questions are being considered. The Renaissance is thought of as producing new movements in art and philosophy, or a new attitude to life. In Troeltsch's very comprehensive work on *Die Soziallehren der Christlichen Kirchen und Gruppen* there is no chapter on the Renaissance and Humanism— as though they had involved no new ethics with a religious foundation. Max Weber speaks only of *protestant* ethics in relation to the "Spirit of Capitalism" and does not mention Erasmus; nor does Tawney.

This view seems to me entirely incorrect. In the first place, can we call "the" Renaissance and Humanism as a whole un-Christian or indifferent as far as religion is concerned? According to Wernle (who is considerably more susceptible to the ideal values of the Renaissance than many others, who would, all the same, willingly endorse

the following view), the Humanist is characterized by "complete attachment to the things of this world, the complete reliance of man on himself, a high self-respect," and this latter quality is immediately identified with *Ruhmsucht* (thirst for glory), and *Selbstsucht* (selfishness); with an entire lack of moral and religious ideals, a limitation to reality and the individual. Such descriptions imply that the fifteenth century Italian had no faith, and this supposed lack is then simply equated with paganism. Undoubtedly many people at this time dared to express their desire for power, gain and fame more boldly, and perhaps also more consciously, than in the "pious" Middle Ages, but was this age therefore more materialistic than that which preceded it?

Whenever we consider civilization we must bear in mind the leaders of cultural life and the real bearers of culture. In the 15th and 16th centuries these were certainly no less "idealists" than before or after, in the sense of being governed by spiritual values, and of being directed towards matters extending far above and beyond their own ego. Although they were more conscious of the rights of the individual as opposed to those of the community, they appreciated the spiritual power of the desire for praise, and measured the values of this world and life not only, and sometimes not at all, by the importance which these values have for an imagined hereafter.

The Humanist was religious in the broad sense of the word, in that he felt himself attached to powers and values outside his own ego. He was—and no distinction need be made here between the Italians and those who carried out similar studies in the countries to the North and West of the Alps—a convinced confessor of the Christian faith, except for a few who were either completely converted by what they found in the writings of the Greeks and Romans, or who evolved still further in the modern direction. We shall have something to say about this second group later. But the majority of Humanists considered themselves positive confessors of Christianity, and these are of greater importance for the spiritual life of the sixteenth century, for its political development, and for the origin of what we call "modern civilization." They are important in so far as the religious views of the majority of the outstanding artists, writers and scholars of the period were under the direct influence of these Humantists with a modern outlook. Most remained or were called Catholic, but— and to this point I will devote particular attention—they were not Catholic in the orthodox sense, and some were Protestant, but not in the Reformation sense. Nor, as is often stated, did they stand midway between the two. On the contrary, while they submitted directly to the dogmas of the Catholic Church or joined one of the evangelical or reformed Churches, they gave an entirely individual interpretation to the dogmas and rites of these churches. This interpretation was not more moderate, but deviated more radically from the views of the Middle Ages, and was thus modern in the sense of being closer to views which are fairly generally accepted at present.

At the time of the Renaissance, i.e. between 1450 and 1560, there took place, as I wish to show, together with the many new things that the Renaissance brought in other fields of spiritual life, a religious reformation which went considerably further than what is usually termed the Reformation. In the six-teenth century (and in the succeeding centuries) we have to distinguish side by side with Catholicism and Protestantism a third religious movement, parallel to both but not between them, and having a more modern aspect. It is a well-defined religious opinion, even if it is not laid down in any confession of faith. I shall call it humanistic religion, because it was principally held by those whom we have long been accustomed to call "Humanists," and because, by shifting attention from God to man, it signifies the beginning of the evolution which, via the Enlightenment, finds its most consistent continuation in what in recent years has been called "Humanism" on the Continent, and "Ethical Culturism" in England. Since it is more radical than the Reformation of Luther and Calvin, and since it was of far-reaching influence on the whole of cultural life, while the influence of the Protestant Reformation, apart from a modified view of the relationship of man to God, was limited to the interrelations of church, state and the individual, I call the one the *major* and the other the *minor* Reformation, aware that by this I am also expressing a personal appraisal, and not only an objective historical one.

Let me indicate in greater detail what I mean here by "major." If in religious history we observe a gradual evolution from the primitive to the modern, we can speak of "backward" and "progressive" phases within it, without labelling any stage in the development as more or less significant. We can indicate, at each point in the evolution, the extent to which it contributed to, or shared, the development as a whole; there can then be determined from a series of facts whether they involved a large or small mutation. Whichever creed we consider to be the true one, we should recognize as historians that neither mediaeval Catholicism nor the view of Luther and Calvin formed a final point, any more than modern Humanism will appear to be a final point. It is not, therefore, a question of *personal* sympathy or appreciation if we find that mediaeval Catholicism is widely separated from the view of life of most people in modern times, and that the ideas which are here described as humanistic religion meant a more important evolutionary advance than what Luther or Calvin taught. For this reason in particular I speak of a "major" Reformation, alongside, and going further than, the "minor" one which is usually described as *the* Reformation of the sixteenth century.

In the sixteenth century two new paths were entered in the evolution from primitive religion to the modern attitude to life and the world. A greater differentiation in religious matters was the result. One path differing only slightly from that which had hitherto been followed, brought an important renewal of the means by which man hopes to gain his salvation. The other saw this salvation itself in a new light, and rejected even more radically the traditional means to it. It was a path whereby the religious element was bound, in the end, to lose its importance, and the philosophical-ethical element to attain exclusive preeminence. The more primitive a religion, the more mysterious is its conception of the sacramental (the way in which man and God stand in relation to one another), and the greater the longing for deliverance from an existence which is felt to be guilty and incomplete. Burckhardt and Dilthey have already seen that a deviation from this attitude took place during the Renaissance: the greater appreciation of earthly life put a philosophical in place of a religious

salvation, since man, conscious of his own worth, considered himself capable of self-deliverance through knowledge and effort. There is then no serious mention either of supernatural mercy or of a supernatural saviour.

Stadelmann, who does not sympathize with this development, sees in it a direct renunciation of the religious element when he says: "Religion is to be found where a hyperindividual reality irresistibly invades being and consciousness, and forces them to adoration and allegiance." He does, however, correctly define the Renaissance view (considered by him as inferior): "This new mode of thought makes of the individual a creator who knows Truth because it is within him, and desires, or should desire, Good as an idea (but not as God). The intellect has become a principle, and has transmuted the reality of the Governor of the world and the Redeemer of the soul to an abstract substance, which by its nature is of the same kind as that which constitutes man."

Here two factors are mentioned which were potent in the thought of the Humanists, and which caused them, even while they retained traditional conformity, to deviate from traditional religion: namely the rational element and the relationship to man. Johannes Kühn accentuates a third factor when he speaks of the "new sense of piety" in those who, in the sixteenth century, no longer thought and felt with the aid of concrete religious ideas, a sense of piety "which lives in a perception and experience of the moral nature and destination of man." Accordingly, ethics are released from theology, or, as I would prefer to put it, theology loses power, since religion is replaced by philosophy and morality. *Eine sittliche Gewissensreligiosität* (a moral religion of the conscience) arises. This, according to Kühn, had the following extremely important consequence for modern culture: "the whole great drama of salvation, with its many institutions, had lost its meaning for the person who no longer understood how to think religiously in a concrete manner." In the end, only providence and consciousness of duty, with its inherent sense of responsibility, remain of the old religious ideas.

In what follows we shall consider the share of the Renaissance in this process: how in Western civilization since the sixteenth century religion evolved from the idea of salvation to that of morality, and how Christian salvation thus generally lost its mystical character and its value, at least for very many people. Most of these people were, however, convinced that they were not in this repudiating Christianity, but rather restoring true Christianity to its original form, and shedding what they regarded as later additions.

PETER MASTEN DUNNE, S.J. (1890–1957)
received his doctorate at the University of California,
Berkeley, and from 1934 to 1957 headed the department
of history at the University of San Francisco. He speaks
of the need for objectivity in writing the history of
the Renaissance and Reformation as one who looks
in from the outside, for his interest was in
Jesuit missions in the southwestern United States.
His major work was *Black Robes in California* (1952).
The selection reprinted here is his presidential
address delivered to the Pacific Historical
Association in December 1956.*

The Need for Objectivity

It is forty-four years since James Harvey Robinson wrote his *New History*. He had probably read Morley and Buckle on Voltaire . . . [who] penned these lines:

I wish to write a history, not of wars, but of society; and to ascertain how men lived in the interior of their families and what were the arts which they commonly cultivated. . . . My object is the history of the human mind and not a mere detail of petty facts; nor am I concerned with the history of great lords. . . . But I want to know what were the steps by which men passed from barbarism to civilization.

Voltaire is thus considered by some to be the father of the New History, and such historians as Niebuhr, Buckle, Grote, and Ranke were among his grateful debtors and followers.

In this brief address it is my purpose to expatiate upon just a single factor or quality of historiography which the New History has brought to the attention of historians, a point which received good attention by James Harvey Robinson and which is in accord with the words of Voltaire: "a history of society" and "of the human mind." This factor concerns the elimination of emotional bias in historical writing. In the past such emotionalism, whether it had its roots in nationalism, philosophy, or religion, has

    * Reprinted from Peter Masten Dunne, S.J., "The Renaissance and Reformation: A Study in Objectivity," *Pacific Historical Review*, XXVI (1957), 107–122. Reprinted by permission of the American Historical Association. Footnotes omitted.

112

disfigured a large amount of historical literature. But let the present generation take heart and be congratulated, for along this line there has been a constant improvement and we have watched American historians such as Ephraim Emerton, Paul Van Dyke, and Will Durant undergo this scientific influence which led them as they lived through the decades to a calmer and therefore a truer appraisal of the past.

I wish to dwell upon one phase of this emotional bias which is not entirely eliminated in the present, namely that bias and those misunderstandings created by differences of religion. Thus my intention explains the title of this paper: "The Renaissance and the Reformation." For this revolutionary period in Europe of four centuries ago, which was the death of the Middle Ages and the birth of modern times, let loose a flood of pent-up and constructive energies, but also created hatreds so acute that they scandalized the non-Christian. . . .

The fierce passions aroused by the religious differences of four hundred years ago are explained by three considerations: the men of that epoch took religion much more to heart than the men of this age; then, uncouthness and ugliness of expression had not been refined by the amenities of an expanding civilization; finally (and I believe this point important), the Renaissance and the Reformation created a break within the Christian family, and family quarrels can become exceedingly acrid. The late Gladys Baker, of respectable Christian family, could study Buddhism, Mohammedanism, Zoroastrianism, or any other religion with no reaction from her friends and family, but when they discovered she was interested in Catholicism loud havoc fell about her ears.

Fifty years ago and beyond it was about the same in Catholic circles, but with historians the bias expressed itself in milder form. The Jesuit historian Anthony Guggenberger published in 1905 three volumes entitled *A General History of the Christian Era*. The book is replete with useful information, but, and I speak generally, we can spot the bias of this writer from his choice of adjectives. . . .

And speaking of adjectives, may I quote from a student of mine of a decade ago reporting on a book he had chosen for collateral reading, Alexander C. Flick's *Decline of the Medieval Church*. The student writes about Flick's account of the quarrel between Pope Boniface VIII and King Philip IV of France:

The author tries to be fair, looking on both sides of the question equally. However, some of his pages are discolored by undesirable and unnecessary anti-Roman bias. For instance, he overdoes the description of some of the popes. This is what he says of Boniface VIII: "He was woefully wanting in common courtesy, human tact and a compromising spirit. He was over-bearing, blunt, implacable, egotistic to an offensive degree, and possessed of a blind, insatiable thirst for power. He was deplorably lacking in wisdom and discernment." [After quoting Flick thus, the student continues:] In referring to members of the Church the author overdoes himself in the use of adjectives. Yet, when writing of the secular rulers, he passes over them lightly, not indulging in a long list of adjectives in regard to their character.

This student had caught the point. Boniface was, indeed, almost all that Flick had described, but Philip IV, with whom Boniface had the resounding quarrel which marked the beginning of the decline of the medieval papacy, was no saint. Strong, derogatory adjectives could be truthfully used concerning him too, but Flick does not employ them. . . .

And so the human understanding is

sometimes a false mirror and with too great ease does it often adopt an opinion which is agreeable to itself. Some thirty years before Flick wrote his two volumes on the decline of the medieval papacy (and it is indeed a work of great merit) it had been dinned into my young ears at school (not in formal history lectures) how the cruel Queen Elizabeth had persecuted and executed the poor Catholics, but never a word did I hear about how "Bloody" Mary burned at the stake the poor Protestants. Yet the record of history is clear. Mary Tudor reigned for five years and her government burned at the stake almost three hundred heretics technically for religion; Elizabeth I reigned forty-five years and had executed not quite two hundred technically for treason. I had heard never a word about Elizabeth's excommunication by Pius V, which automatically made all Catholics rebels (though actually those in England remained loyal), or about the plots, the Babington plot, the Ridolphi plot, and others, fomented by Catholics abroad, or of the activities of the Jesuit Robert Persons plotting to have some Catholic princess, even a Spanish one, displace Elizabeth. For as the reformers plotted against Mary Tudor's government so did exiled Catholics plot against that of Elizabeth. A century ago, or even a half-century ago, before Creighton and Ranke and Pastor and Grisar, it could be said that almost no historian told the whole story of this reformation period, and their narratives were charged with partisanship and emotion. Protestants told their side of the story and Catholics told their side. Hardly anyone seemed to be intellectually detached enough to tell the whole story. Therefore we were fed with legends black and white.

Honor to the honesty of the president of our guild, Lyman Thorndike, for his frank admissions concerning his propagation of black legends about the Borgia pope Alexander VI. Writing in the *Commonweal* for December 17, 1925, Thorndike has the following:

In most works in English on the period, Pope Alexander VI has hitherto been depicted in strong colors as an inhuman monster, exceeded only by Caesar Borgia, commonly reputed to be his son. On looking over, for example, some notes taken sixteen or seventeen years ago in connection with a course that I was giving to undergraduates upon the renaissance, I find such assertions as that he would sell benefices, poison the recipients, and then sell the church offices over again, gratifying simultaneously his cruelty and his avarice. That he had a passionately sensual temperament, kept a harem in the Vatican, and was swayed by an almost insane weakness for his illegitimate children. That he bought the papal election, and that he probably died as a result of taking by mistake the poison he had intended for others. As for Caesar, that he once stabbed a minion of the Pope in Alexander's very arms, and would shoot criminals down in a courtyard with bow and arrow for sport.

Thorndike implied that all, or most, of this is legend, as indeed most of it is. Goodness knows, Alexander VI was bad and wicked enough and no Catholic historian now tries to whitewash him. Imbart de la Tour grouped with him Sixtus IV and Innocent VIII as the three evil geniuses of the Church, and Hilaire Belloc has averred that the Church has not yet recovered from the blow delivered it by this scandalous personality. But the New History has learned, setting aside emotional prejudices, to sift the flying chaff of legend from the golden grains of truth.

In English historiography the closer we approach the age of the Reformation the hotter becomes the emotion and the more extreme becomes the literary phrasing. Superlatives and accumulated strong adjectives are a clear betrayal. Here is a passage on the history of the popes from John Mills, an English historian, writing in 1757: "I have no interest to praise or blame the See of Rome. . . . Avarice, ambition, sacrilege, perjury, absolute contempt for everything sacred, the most amazing dissoluteness, every species of debauchery in excess, a total depravity and corruption of doctrine and morals characterize the history of the Papacy."

If we realize what heat of emotions and passions was stirred by the religious revolt of the sixteenth century, we shall hardly be surprised at the enduring quality of legends then begun, especially when, during the reign of Elizabeth I, very much as the result of the conflict with Spain, English Protestantism became identified with English nationalism. Pope Pius V's excommunication of Elizabeth in 1570, when she was rising to the height of her popularity in England, did but kindle additional flames. Thenceforward, at least technically, to be a Catholic was to be a traitorous Englishman. Such tensioned emotionalism was carried down through the decades and through the centuries in a famous book: *Fox's Book of Martyrs.* Generations of Englishmen were fed upon this book as with their mother's milk; it was read daily in the homes together with the Bible, and with the Bible almost up to the twentieth century it could be seen, chained for reading, in the vestibules of village parish churches. From this source parsons were supplied with material for their discourses. Here was part of the religious sustenance of a whole people, and the fact that the edition I have used is that of 1875, whereas it first appeared in 1563, demonstrates the permanence of its influence. As

Father Philip Hughes wrote recently: "Fox's book ended all hope of popular support of the old religion in England." And to quote James F. Mozley: "If anything could make England Protestant forever it would be the memory of the Marian terror, and [Fox] desired to burn his dreadful history into the minds of his countrymen both high and low." The book was a Pegasus breathing flames from either nostril. . . .

William Tyndale, like all the other English reformers with the possible exception of Thomas Cranmer, was of similar vehemence. Tyndale was burned at the stake as a heretic under Henry VIII after the latter's break with Rome. Concerning him, Philip Hughes has this rather strong passage:

Along with Tyndale's moving exhortations to charity and to love of enemies, to fortitude and the confidence that God will bring his own safely through, there is the bitterest hatred everywhere evident, not only for the abuses of the old system and for the clerics responsible for these, but for every feature of Catholic belief and practice. There is biting ridicule and reckless misrepresentation; wild, unscrupulous, hate-inspired all-embracing railery, reviling and insults for everything dear to the religious mind of the time, save only the name of Christ himself.

Here we have the reasons why the reviewer R. E., in the *New Republic* (April 21, 1952), of Harry Emerson Fosdick's *Great Voices of the Reformation* could speak of "the fury and savagery of sixteenth century Protestantism."

Such was quite generally the language of the reformers, and it was used not only against the adherents of the old religion, but against all who disagreed with them. The reformer John Philpot considered the early English heretics, called Arians at that time, as "persons of a beastly understanding"; they are "flaming fire-brands of hell," the "vile seeds of the serpent" and "inordinate swine." "Upon all that have love and fellowship with such . . . the same damnation shall fall . . . as is due to the wicked heretics." Philpot is sorry his spittle has not the power to blind the Arian. So it was with other leaders: Tyndale, Latimer, Jewel, Hooper. Edward VI had Anabaptists and so-called Donatists burned at the stake, Latimer approving. In Geneva Calvin wrote: "Whoever shall now contend that it is unjust to put heretics and blasphemers to death will knowingly and willingly incur their very guilt." And in Scotland John Knox was explaining to Christians the proper way to hate.

It is universally acknowledged, for the record is there, that those who are the leaders of revolution are the more vigorous in action and the more reckless in accusation than the traditional group against whom the revolution is activated. So it was during the Age of the Reformation. Pope Pius V's bull of excommunication of Elizabeth in 1570 is comparatively mild. I quote the strongest passage: "But the number of the impious has grown powerful to such an extent that no place on earth is left that these do not endeavor to corrupt with their most evil doctrines, with the aid among others of the servant of infamy, Elizabeth, the pretended queen of England, to whom as to an asylum the most wicked men have found refuge." Not so, however, Cardinal Allen, leader of the English exiles on the Continent. He had prepared a document to be broadcast in England at the time of the proposed landing of the Spanish Armada. Its language sinks to the level of most of the above quotations. Elizabeth is "an incestuous bastard, begotten and born in sin of an infamous courtesan." There

follows a wealth of abuse concerning the details of her private morals and public policy. Catholics are invited to rise against this "infamous, depraved, accursed, excommunicate heretic; the very shame of her sex and princely name; the chief spectacle of sin and abomination in this our age; the only poison, calamity and destruction of our noble Church and country." The English Jesuit Persons, who gave occasion to much anti-Jesuit-ism in England by his political activities in Rome and at the court in Spain, was goaded by the language of the reformers against him to remark, rather mildly, about one of his maligners: "He is of such queer and misshapen visage that he looketh three ways at once." He meant, doubtless, that the man was cross-eyed. . . .

Shall we pass on to Germany, so ripe for the revolution of the early sixteenth century with so many of her leaders furious against Rome, that Rome which was the seat of the Papacy and which since Sixtus IV (1471–1484) seemed to have lost the universal view of a united Christendom and to have sunk to the level of just another Italian principality; of a Papacy which was bleeding Germany by its exorbitant fees and taxes; of a Papacy whose court had become foul with corruption; of a Papacy whose clergy throughout Europe was largely venal and immoral? Indeed the abuses and corruptions within the old Church were intolerable. Something had to happen, either reform or revolution. Reform did not take place, so revolution flamed forth.

Protestantism was born when Martin Luther so speedily and so unexpectedly acquired so great a following. We cannot be surprised at such a development. Cardinal Cesarini, papal legate to Germany a century before, wrote to Pope

Eugenius IV warning him that unless the German clergy were reformed another and more deadly revolution than the Hussite revolt in Bohemia would break out. Reform did not come: Martin Luther did. Many thought Luther would reform the Church; some of the princes had an eye on the broad acres of abbeys and bishoprics; with still others it was the new nationalism, young and vigorous and resenting the rule of Italians even over the Church. . . .

Shall we look into Luther's language and examine the origins of the black legend which he created about the whole of Catholicism? We cannot in the interests of historical truth lift him out of his age and judge him by present standards, but even in an uncouth age William S. Lilly considered him easily the prince "in the art of fierce flagellation and fetid foulness." To Luther Rome was the filth of iniquity, and the Pope was Anti-Christ and the Whore of Babylon. Some other passages, for example, from his letters and his *Table Talk*, are unfit to print. Yet, apart from his significant strength of leadership, he had humane qualities which made him admired and loved by those who knew him well. And before Luther died Rome had already begun those processes which would lead to complete reformation from within. The Jesuits, soul of the Counter-Revolution, had been approved in 1540, and in 1545, the year before Luther's death, there were held the first sessions of the reforming Council of Trent. The evil that men do lives after them; partisanship forgets the good, and the legend floats down the centuries.

There is a black legend current among those of the old religion about Luther himself, which has been carried on by the uninstructed, yes and by those who should have known better. None of his great qualities are remembered in the legend; only his strong and sometimes foul language and, like Calvin, he is said to have died a miserable death. In the older days before the New History, attitudes were not much changed from those of the age of the Reformation. Catholics painted Luther black; Protestants painted him white. But as with most human beings, this powerful personality was neither white nor black; he was a shade of gray. It is the historian's job, with serene and unbiased mind, to try to catch and depict the exact shade. . . .

The Counter-Reformation begins and develops and spreads. Its most important, but not its only, motivating force in the field was that mobile order of Jesuits. Ronald Hilton has written that they too, have suffered from a black legend. They were sly and cunning men, bloated with greed and ambition, corrupters of youth and propagators of the principle that the end justifies the means, according to the olden partisan story. Many other black legends were developed in this connection and on the other hand, within the Order, many white ones, too. I have a pamphlet on my shelves, published in London in 1679 and "Printed for Henry Brome at the Gun in St. Paul's Churchyard." Its title runs thus: "The Jesuits Unmasked: or Politick Observations upon the Ambitious Pretentions and Subtle Intreagues of that Cunning Society." From the title one can judge the contents. Among other things the author says that one is to take notice "that there are three sorts of Jesuits, or Ignatians." The first consists of lay persons of both sexes; the second only of men, some priests, some laymen; "The third sort of politick Jesuits is of those in whose hands resides the main authority that sits at the stern of their Order. . . ." This pamphlet demonstrates the kind of national hysteria which had taken hold of England at that time and which led to the absurdities and injustices of the "famous scare" of the popish plot of 1678, the year just previous to the date of the pamphlet. . . .

About South America, another historian has written: The Jesuits were "willing enough to support themselves at the sweat of others' brows, and even by others' blood." And concerning colonial Maryland: The situation was aggravated by the attitude of the Jesuits "who seemed to be determined to acquire great areas of land and set up an independent spiritual domain, with the separate canon law and great temporal power under the suzerainty, not of Baltimore, but of the Pope." These three assertions are not supported by documentary evidence; indeed, the documentary evidence runs in the opposite direction. The last two quotes belong to the mid-twentieth century and are of reputable historians. Tradition dies hard. Shall we call such statements with their errors and their emotional animus the fag end of a black legend extending up into the present day?

Human nature being what it is, no calm and philosophical historian should be surprised at all of this, nor should he lose his poise and equanimity, no matter to what school he belongs. James Harvey Robinson gives the answer: "Protestants soon realized that the new Jesuit Order was their most powerful and dangerous enemy. Their apprehensions produced a bitter hatred which blinded them to the high purposes of the founder of the Order and led them to attribute an evil purpose to every act of the Jesuits." . . .

Some writers of the opposing camp wrote about the Jesuits without animus,

exaggeration or legend, even with praise. Such were Francis Bacon and John Selden in England and Montaigne in France. . . .

The historical weed of legend springs from the fertile soil of human inaccuracy, human imagination, human partisanship, human passions. After all, the proverb has it right: *Errare humanum est:* To err is human. Our guild of historians in this matter of emotional partisanship has encouragingly and very notably improved within the last half-century. Since nothing human is ever perfect we can always strive for more intelligent attitudes. Our students in the classroom, the readers of our books, depend upon us to give them as accurate a picture of the past as is humanly possible. Our techniques have improved tremendously; our emotional attitudes have been measurably eliminated, difficult as it is to throw off a tradition; our calm detachment, even with regard to the controversial period we have been speaking of, has been of admirable quality as the most recent publications, with few exceptions, abundantly show. This is all to the good so that we can take encouragement. . . .

The true historian abhors a narrative which is sicklied over with pale apologetics or vitiated by the distortions of propaganda or the contortions of prejudice and bias. I close with a statement made by one of the past presidents of our guild, Samuel E. Morison. In his presidential address of 1950, he said: "No person without an inherent loyalty to truth, a high degree of intellectual honesty, and a sense of balance can be a great or even a good historian. Truth about the past is the essence of history and historical biography."

Suggested Additional Readings

Ample supplies of material are available for those who desire to read further concerning the Reformation. Not only have historians over the past fifty to sixty years written voluminously on the subject, but sociologists, economists, and especially theologians have poured out books, articles, and new editions of sources. One only has to glance through the bibliographies that have appeared recently to realize how much attention is at the present time being devoted to this period. Consequently, one can only indicate briefly a few of the avenues a student may follow, by referring to some of the works that have appeared over the past two decades.

Probably the most important general bibliography is that which the Commission Internationale d'Histoire Ecclésiastique Comparée has published serially since 1958. It lists by countries all works dealing with the Reformation that appeared between 1940 and 1955. However, the lists are unclassified, and this is only partially compensated for by the subject indices. A more usable, because shorter and classified, bibliography is that published in *The Review and Expositor*, vol. LXIV (1967), "Studies of the Sixteenth-Century Protestant Reformation: The Literature in English, 1946–1966," by James Leo Garrett. The second edition of Karl Schottenloher: *Bibliographie zur Deutsche Geschichte in Zeitalter der Glaubenspaltung, 1517–1585* (7 vols.; Stuttgart, 1956–1960), gives a very complete bibliography of writings on Luther to 1960, and includes considerable material on the other reformers. D. A. Erichson's bibliography of works on Calvin published to 1900, *Bibliographia Calviniana* (Nieuwkoop, Netherlands) was reissued in 1960 and has been extended to 1959 by Wilhelm Niesel's *Calvin Bibliographie, 1901–1959* (Munich, 1961). Various review articles have also appeared in recent years dealing with the Reformation. Among them are Roland H. Bainton, "Interpretations of the Reformation," *American Historical Review*, XLVI (1960), 74–84; E. A. Dowey, "Studies in Calvin and Calvinism since 1955," *Church History*, XXIX (1960), 187–204; J. Dillenberger, "Major Volumes and Selected Periodical Literature in Lutheran Studies," *Church History*, XXXI (1961), 61–88; C. Krahn, "Menno Simons Research," *Church History*, XXX (1961), 473–481; and G. W. Locher, "The Change in the Understanding of Zwingli in Recent Research," *Church History*, XXXIV (1965), 3–25. Many useful bibliographies may be found also in various general works on the Reformation, while the new literature on the subject is reviewed each quarter in *Archiv für Reformationsgeschichte*.

One thing particularly noticeable in the last few decades has been the publication or republication of the collected works of many of the reformers. Luther's writings newly translated into English have nearly all appeared in a fifty-five volume collection published by Concordia Press, St. Louis. The Brunswick edition of Calvin has been reprinted and can be obtained on microform (Micro-card Editions). Zwingli-Verlag of Zürich is now publishing the works of Zwingli. Similar projects are under way for the reissuing of various Anabaptists' writings. Probably the most useful set for the average student, however, is the "Library of Christian Classics" (London and Philadelphia), of which Volumes XIV to XXVI provide

English translations of the most significant writings of all the major reformers. One might add two other collections: G. Wolf, *Quellenkunde der deutschen Reformationsgeschichte* (3 vols.; Nieuwkoop, Netherlands, 1965) and H. J. Hillerbrand, *The Reformation: A Narrative History Related by Contemporary Observers and Participants* (New York, 1964); both provide interesting and useful, although by no means complete, materials.

In view of the appearance of all these collections, it is hardly strange that the past two or three decades have witnessed the publication of many histories of the Reformation and collections of essays on the movement. Of the general histories, H. Hauser and H. Renaudet, *Les Débuts de l'Age Modern* (Paris, 1956) still holds a place of importance, and Will Durant, *The Reformation* (New York, 1957) enjoys considerable popularity although at times one might well call in question some of its statements both of fact and interpretation. The *New Cambridge Modern History: The Reformation* (vol. II; London, 1958) is considerably different from the volume on the Reformation in the older Cambridge series. Although in some ways it is an improvement, in that it deals with various aspects of historical context ignored by the original volume, it does not give as thorough a treatment of the Reformation itself. Some earlier works on the Reformation such as Charles Beard, *The Reformation of the Sixteenth Century* (Ann Arbor, Mich., 1962), originally published in 1883, have now appeared in reprint, while so many new monographs covering the whole movement are now available in both hard and soft covers that one cannot hope to mention more than a few: H. J. Grimm, *The Reformation Era, 1500–1650* (New York, 1954); Roland H. Bainton, *The Reformation of the Sixteenth Century* (Boston, 1952); G. L. Mosse, *The Reformation* (New York, 1963); G. R. Elton, *Reformation Europe, 1517–1559* (London, 1963); and Owen Chadwick, *The Reformation* (Harmondsworth, England, 1964). Even Roman Catholics such as H. Daniel-Rops (*The Protestant Reforma-*

tion; New York, 1961) are writing accounts of the religious upheaval although with a perspective somewhat different from that of the Protestants.

Among the collections of essays perhaps two of the best are Wilhelm Pauck, *The Heritage of the Reformation* (Glencoe, Ill., 1961) and *Reformation Studies, Essays in Honor of Roland H. Bainton* edited by F. H. Littell (Richmond, 1962).

Along with the general surveys of the period, there have appeared a number of histories of the Reformation as it affected particular nations. Johannes Lortz, *Die Reformation in Deutschland* (2 vols.; Freiburg, Germany, 1948) deals with the German Reformation from a Roman Catholic perspective, and Volume I of Hajo Holborn, *History of Germany* (New York, 1961) is also largely devoted to the Reformation in Germany. Philip Hughes has written a very detailed study of *The Reformation in England* (3 vols.; New York, 1961) in which he sets forth the Roman Catholic view of the movement in that country. In *The Scottish Reformation* (London, 1960) Gordon Donaldson of Edinburgh University has sought to prove that the Scottish Reformation was really episcopalian in intent. There are also many histories of the origins of Protestantism in various other countries, but they often give the impression that while they devote close study to their subjects, they have a particular axe to grind or seek to prove some point in connection with a contemporary church controversy or for some political, economic, or social theory.

Biographies of the reformers have been written in large numbers. Luther in particular has come in for extensive study on all sides. One of the most important devoted to him is that of Roland H. Bainton, *Here I Stand* (New York, 1950) which, however, stresses primarily the early part of his career. R. H. Fife, *The Revolt of Martin Luther* (New York, 1957); Heinrich Boehmer, *Road to Reformation* translated by J. W. Doberstein and T. G. Tappert (Philadelphia, 1946); and E. H. Erikson, *Young Man Luther* (New York, 1958) all likewise seek to explain his development as a reformer but do not attempt to cover the story of his whole life. No comparable studies have been devoted to Calvin, probably because Doumergue, *Jean Calvin* (7 vols.; 1899–1927), deals with the subject so exhaustively. A number of short popular biographies have been written, however, among them Jean Cadier, *Calvin—L'Homme que Dieu A Dompté* (Geneva, 1958) and Thea B. Van Halsema, *This was John Calvin* (Grand Rapids, Mich., 1959). The latter is a study of Calvin as a man rather than as a reformer. There are biographies of Zwingli: O. Farner, *Huldrych Zwingli* (3 vols.; Zurich, 1943, 1946, 1960) and J. H. Rillier, *Zwingli, The Third Man of the Reformation*, translated by H. Knight (London, 1964). Works on other reformers include: J. Ridley, *Thomas Cranmer* (Oxford, 1962); on John Knox, Geddes MacGregor, *The Thundering Scot* (Philadelphia, n.d.) and Elizabeth Whitley, *Plain Mr. Knox* (Richmond, 1960); A. Bouvier, *Henri Bullinger, le Successeur de Zwingli* (Paris, 1940); C. L. Manschreck, *Melanchthon, The Quiet Reformer* (Nashville, Tenn., 1958); and C. Hopf, *Martin Bucer and the English Reformation* (Oxford, England, 1946). Many of the biographical works seek to deal with their subjects from some particular point of view or with some aspect of their reforming activities and labors.

Other writers, and there are many, have made studies of the thought of the reformers in general, of the thought of one reformer, or even of one aspect of a reformer's teachings. Henry Strohl has written *La Pensée de la Réforme* (Paris, 1951) as a general introduction to the reformers' teachings while Heinrich Bornkamm in *The Heart of the Reformation Faith*, translated by J. W. Doberstein (New York, 1963), has set forth what he feels to be the essentials of sixteenth-century Protestant beliefs. The latter work at times tends to interpret the reformers in terms of twentieth-century German theological categories. Such bias is of course always possible and one finds it wherever one turns. Among the general studies

of Luther, H. H. W. Kramm, *The Theology of Martin Luther* (London, 1947) is one of the most useful analyses of the reformer's thought; Regin Prenter, *Spiritus Creator* (Philadelphia, 1953) is a study of Luther's concept of the Holy Spirit; and Gordon Rupp, *The Righteousness of God* (London, 1953) deals with selected aspects of his theology. In Calvin studies, Wilhelm Niesel, *The Theology of Calvin* (London, 1956), François Wendel, *Calvin: The Origins and Development of His Religious Thought* (New York, 1963), and J. T. McNeill, *The History and Character of Calvinism* (New York, 1957) seek to give an overall view. There are however, so many studies of Calvin's individual doctrines that one simply cannot enumerate them. To a lesser extent this is true also of material about the other reformers.

In dealing with these works one must always be conscious of the theological background and views of the authors. Not infrequently a study of Luther, Calvin, Thomas Münzer, Menno Simons, or some other reformer is aimed at proving that some specific point of view, or some particular doctrine or doctrinal perspective, finds its origins in the Reformation. This entails constant vigilance on the part of the student.

Many historians have written recently on the relation of the Reformation to sixteenth-century culture. The connection between Reformation and the Renaissance has always intrigued many and still does. The reprinting of earlier works such as Karl Holl, *The Cultural Significance of the Reformation* (New York, 1959) and Johann Huizinga, *Erasmus and the Age of Reformation* (New York, 1957) indicate this. The recent work of A. G. Dickens, *Reformation and Society in Sixteenth-Century Europe* (London, 1966) provides a useful summary of what is known about this subject, although it offers no new synthesis. Other more detailed studies such as R. M. Kingdon, *Geneva and the Coming of the Wars of Religion in France* (Geneva, 1956), William Monter, *Calvin's Geneva* (Neukirchen, Germany, 1957) and Gerald Strauss, *Nuremberg in the 16th Century*

(New York, 1966) are but a few of the works dealing with the socio-political background of sixteenth-century religious developments. Works such as E. H. Harbison, *The Christian Scholar in the Age of the Reformation* (New York, 1956) and H. C. Porter, *Reformation and Reaction in Tudor Cambridge* (London, 1958) deal with another aspect of the interaction between the Reformation and its environment.

One facet of recent studies on the Reformation has been Roman Catholic–Protestant relations. This matter has of course always been considered in works on the Catholic, or Counter, Reformation, as for instance in Daniel-Rops, *The Catholic Reformation* (New York, 1963). Two useful works in this general area are: J. Lecler, *Toleration and the Reformation* (2 vols.; New York, 1960)

and F. Richter, *Martin Luther and Ignatius Loyola* (Westminster, Md., 1960). These works do not merely deal with the subject in an abstract or academic manner, but reflect the current interest in the contemporary Roman Catholic–Protestant dialogue.

As one studies the voluminous literature on the Reformation, one soon comes to realize that in the minds of many the issues involved are still very much live options. But the various and conflicting approaches and interpretations also reveal what has been called the "ambiguity" of history. Was the Reformation "a good thing" or "a bad thing"? One's evaluation will depend largely upon one's own presuppositions, and the student must decide what his presuppositions are, so that he may have a profitable dialogue with the works he is reading.

Date Due

SEP 2 6 1984	APR 2 5 1989	
OCT 1 0 1984	NOV 2 0 1990	
	NOV 2 3 1991	
DEC 0 1 1984	NOV 1 1 1993	
MAR 2 ,	NOV 1 9 1995	
MAR 2 7 1985	DEC - 2 1995	
NOV 2 0 1985	FEB 1 3 1997	
JAN 2 3 1986	FEB 1 1 1997	
MAR 0 4 1986	MAR 1 1 1998	
JAN 3 0	MAR 2 4 1998	
DEC 5 1987	NOV 0 8 1998	
FEB 0 2 1989	NOV 0 1 1998	
FEB 1 7 1989	OCT 2 1 2003	
MAR 1 3 1989	NOV 1 3 2003	
MAR 2 6 1989		
APR 1 0 1989		

BRODART, INC.   Cat. No. 23 233   Printed in U S A